AP ENGLISH
LITERATURE AND COMPOSITION
CRASH COURSE

By Dawn Hogue

D0377523

Research & Education Association
Visit our website at: www.rea.com

Research & Education Association
61 Ethel Road West
Piscataway, New Jersey 08854
E-mail: info@rea.com

AP ENGLISH LITERATURE AND COMPOSITION CRASH COURSE

Printed in the United States of America

Library of Congress Control Number 2010920834

ISBN-13: 978-0-7386-0782-5
ISBN-10: 0-7386-0782-7

REA® is a registered trademark of Research & Education Association, Inc.

AP ENGLISH LITERATURE AND COMPOSITION CRASH COURSE TABLE OF CONTENTS

ABOUT THIS BOOK

REA's *AP English Literature and Composition Crash Course* is the first book of its kind for the last-minute studier or any AP student who wants a quick refresher on the course. The *Crash Course* is based on a careful analysis of the AP English Literature and Composition Course Description outline and actual AP test questions.

Written by an AP English teacher, our easy-to-read format gives students a crash course in the major elements of literature and provides expert advice on writing essays. The targeted review chapters prepare students for the exam by focusing on the important topics tested on the AP English Literature and Composition exam.

Unlike other test preps, REA's *AP English Literature and Composition Crash Course* gives you a review specifically focused on what you really need to study in order to ace the exam. The review chapters offer you a concise way to learn all the important AP material before the test.

The introduction discusses the keys for success and shows you strategies to help you build your overall point score. Part Two is an overview of the basic elements of literature. The chapters focus on fiction, poetry, and language, and provide a handy summary of literary periods, authors, and concepts.

In Part Three, the author shows you how to interpret reading passages and explains literary themes. Part Four is devoted exclusively to essay writing. Our review of essay basics and an in-depth analysis of an essay prompt will help you improve your composition skills.

Part Five gives you expert advice on how to master the multiple-choice section of the AP English Literature and Composition exam. The author explains the types of questions asked in the multiple-choice section, and offers strategies for success that will help you raise your point score.

No matter how or when you prepare for the AP English Literature and Composition exam, REA's *Crash Course* will show you how to study efficiently and strategically, so you can boost your score!

If you would like to assess your test-readiness for the AP English Literature and Composition exam after studying this *Crash Course*, you can access a complimentary full-length AP English Literature and Composition practice exam at *www.rea.com/crashcourse*. This true-to-format test includes detailed explanations of answers and will help you identify your strengths and weaknesses before taking the actual AP exam.

Good luck on your AP English Literature and Composition exam!

ABOUT OUR AUTHOR

Dawn Hogue has taught all levels of high school English and is currently an AP English teacher for the Sheboygan Falls School District, Sheboygan Falls, Wisconsin. She has received numerous awards and recognition for her role in the classroom, including selection as Teacher of the Year by the Sheboygan Falls Faculty Association in 2000.

Ms. Hogue received her B.A. in English, graduating Summa Cum Laude, from Lakeland College, Sheboygan, Wisconsin. She earned her M.A. in Education from Lakeland College, Sheboygan, Wisconsin and her M.S. in Educational Leadership from Cardinal Stritch University, Milwaukee, Wisconsin.

She is interested in promoting technology and web resources in the classroom and maintains a website (www.mshogue.com) for that purpose.

ACKNOWLEDGMENTS

In addition to our author, we would like to thank Larry B. Kling, Vice President, Editorial, for his overall guidance, which brought this publication to completion Pam Weston, Vice President, Publishing for setting the quality standards for production integrity and managing the publication to completion; Diane Goldschmidt, Senior Editor, for editorial project management; Alice Leonard, Senior Editor, for preflight editorial review; Rachel DiMatteo, Graphic Artist, for page designs, and Weymouth Design, for designing our cover.

We also extend our special thanks to Kathy Caratozzolo of Caragraphics, for typesetting this edition.

PART I:

INTRODUCTION

Keys for Success
on the AP English Literature and Composition Exam

It was July 1995, after my first year teaching AP English. My son had taken a phone message from one of my students who was very excited to tell me the results of her exam. He said, "Mom, one of your students called and said she got a four on some test." Confused by what appeared to be a very low score, he then asked, "Is that good?" I smiled. Not good. It is great!

In This Chapter

Overview

Structure of the Exam

Scoring of the Exam

Estimating Your Score

What to Know About Exam Day

OVERVIEW

The Odyssey by Homer is considered the first epic poem. The first English novel is often said to be *Robinson Crusoe* by Daniel Defoe written in 1719. Walt Whitman, who lived and wrote in the 1800s, is said to be the father of free verse. There is a long, complex history of world literature, and there is so much to know. Even college literature professors do not study the entirety of the literary field but instead specialize in a particular aspect, such as British Romanticism. You are not expected to know it all, either. How could you?

The AP English Literature and Composition Exam (AP Lit) presents many challenges, and even if you had read every book ever written, you might not be prepared for what is in store for you. So, knowing that you can't study it all, the purpose of this book is to give you the most important keys to success.

In the chapters that follow, you will get content specific help, tips for success, and general insight about what you need to know. This chapter gives you a glimpse into the structure and scoring of the exam as well as general ways to prepare yourself for the big day in May.

STRUCTURE OF THE EXAM

Part I: 55 multiple-choice questions in 60 minutes, 45% of the total score

Part II: three essays in 120 minutes, 55% of the total score

Test proctors will give a short break between Part I and Part II. Your AP English Literature and Composition instructor is not allowed to proctor your exam.

SCORING OF THE EXAM

The multiple-choice section is scored by machine.

The three essays are scored by AP readers in early June. Readers include college professors and experienced AP English teachers, who meet for this purpose. These readers work in teams to read and score essays using scoring guides provided to them. Your essay is not identified by name or geographical location. Every effort is made to ensure objectivity and fairness in assessing essays.

The scores from Part I and II are combined to create a composite score. See how to estimate your score later in this chapter.

Scores are reported to students and designated colleges in July.

AP SCORE SCALE

5	Extremely well-qualified
4	Well-qualified
3	Qualified
2	Possibly qualified
1	Not qualified

Qualification is to receive college credit or advanced placement.

In its information to AP students, the College Board writes: "You may be very surprised to see that your composite score can be approximately two-thirds of the total possible score and you could still earn a grade of 5! " Earning that score on other exams might translate to an "F" at worst and a "D" at best. In other words, you do not have to get all the multiple-choice questions right or write perfect essays to get a high score on the exam.

In the 2006 figures reported by the College Board, 62.1% of all students who took the exam scored a 3 or higher. And while fewer than 10% of students scored a 5 in 2006 (which says a bit about the difficulty of the exam), you should focus on the high number who passed. A 3, 4, or 5 will earn you college credits. (Check with your intended colleges for their AP credit policy.)

2006: ENGLISH LITERATURE GRADE DISTRIBUTIONS

	English Lit./Comp	
Examination Grade	Number of Test Takers Achieving Score	Percent of Test Takers Receiving Score
5	19,890	7.1
4	58,490	20.8
3	96,309	34.3
2	83,702	29.8
1	22,720	8.1
Number of Students	281,111	
3 or Higher / %	174,689	62.1
Mean Grade	2.89	
Standard Deviation	1.05	

ESTIMATING YOUR SCORE

The following form is intended to help you estimate your score when using practice exams. It can only give a general prediction and should not be taken too seriously as an indicator of your potential success. For one thing, if you are scoring your own essays, you may be too hard on yourself. Also, ranges for composite scores can change from year to year as the exam itself changes.

Part I: Multiple-Choice

_____ − = _____ × 1.1321 = _____
(number correct)   (¼ x _____   (your weighted
                         number wrong)   score for Part I)

Part II: Essays

Essay 1: _____ × 3.3333 = _____ (do not round up)

Essay 2: _____ × 3.3333 = _____ (do not round up)

Essay 3: _____ × 3.3333 = _____ (do not round up)

Add the three essay scores = _____
                              (your weighted
                              score for Part II)

Estimating Your Composite Score:

_____ + _____ = _____
(weighted score   (weighted score   (your composite
   Part I)   Part II)   score)

Translating your composite score into an AP Grade:

Composite Score	AP Grade
102–150	5
91–101	4
71–90	3
43–70	2
0–42	1

WHAT TO KNOW ABOUT EXAM DAY

What you can (should have) and cannot have in the exam room:

Yes	No
Several no. 2 pencils, sharpened, with good erasers	Cell phones, mp3 players, or any other electronic device, including calculators
One or two reliable blue or black pens; avoid pens that clump or bleed	Cameras or other recording devices
A watch, so you can monitor your time	Books, including dictionaries
Your social security number	Scratch paper
Water (No bottles with paper labels are allowed.)	Notes you've made in advance
	Highlighters

Preparing yourself personally:

1. Eat well in the weeks prior to the exam. Get used to eating breakfast, so that you can eat a good breakfast on exam day (the AP Lit exam is generally scheduled in the morning). A good breakfast for your brain consists of fruit, lean protein, and complex carbohydrates. Also, drink water not sugared drinks.

2. Get your sleep and not just the night before the exam. Establish good sleep patterns in the weeks prior to the exam. Teens typically do not get enough sleep. Aim for 8–9 hours a night.

3. Wake up early enough to be fully awake and ready to go on exam day. Set your alarm so you don't oversleep. You don't want to be groggy.

4. Caffeine or energy drinks may help you to be more alert, but overdoing them can make you jittery and

make it harder for you to focus. If you are not used to caffeine, you shouldn't have any on exam day.

5. Wear comfortable clothes and shoes on the day of the exam. Prepare for fluctuations in room temperature by wearing layers that you can adjust.

See more in Chapter 2 about what you can do to prepare for exam day.

Students' Tools:
What You Bring
to Your Own Success

OVERVIEW

Any study text is useless if you don't pair it your best intentions. This brief chapter simply outlines what you can do to enhance your own success.

A STATE OF MIND: THE THREE D'S

DESIRE:

This book can only help so much. You have to want to be successful. Your desire to do well must translate into your determination and diligence. But also, your desire must be coupled with a positive and energetic attitude. You have chosen this task because you desire to push yourself. It won't be easy, but most things worthy of our time are not easy.

DETERMINATION:

Whether you are using this book on its own, or along with a structured AP course, you have a lot to accomplish. No book or teacher can do for you what you need to do for yourself. You must be resolute in your determination to accomplish your goals.

DILIGENCE:

You have to keep at it, even when things get tough.

Make a bracelet to wear that displays the three D's to remind you how important your state of mind is. If you ever feel like slacking, your bracelet can remind you to put forth your best effort.

A MATTER OF TIME

You may have heard the saying, "What's worth doing, is worth doing well." This is also true for your preparation for the AP Lit exam—it's worth doing well! It will be very difficult for you to literally cram all you need to know in a short period of time. The information and tips you get in this book will help you to focus and prepare for your exam. However, it is best if you start early enough to really learn what you need to know. Except for some literary terms, there is little in this text that you can actually memorize. Instead, you need to develop your reading, writing, and thinking skills.

SUGGESTED STRATEGIES FOR USING THIS BOOK

1. Read the entire book, noting which topics or chapters will require the most study time. Focus on what you need to know instead of what you already know.

2. Make a goal sheet, listing specific tasks for the upcoming months. For example,

- read three novels and two plays and fill out a *Remembering Major Works* form for each one (see Chapter 4).

- practice annotating all the texts you read.

3. Good goals have time limits, so be sure to say when you plan to meet your goals.

4. Re-read this book as often as necessary to reinforce ideas. Most people will not remember everything they read the first time.

5. Make a short list of the five most important skills you need to improve before test time, such as reading complex texts or understanding figurative language. Find ways to practice those skills.

6. Form an AP Lit study team with friends who will be taking the exam. Learn from each other. Here are some reasons to form a study team:

- Team members can quiz each other on subject terms.

- Members can share essays to review them. Peer review can help team members to see strengths and weaknesses in their writing. They can also learn from the reading of each other's work.

- Members who choose to read the same books, can discuss them, which helps everyone to understand a text more completely.

7. If you get frustrated, try these strategies:

- Analyze the reason for your frustration. Why are you frustrated? What can you do to alleviate your frustration?

- Take a short break to refocus: go for a walk outdoors, with no headphones. Let nature (or the city) help you get out of yourself for a while.

- Talk to your study group and vent. Then, together, find ways to get back on track.

- Ask your teacher for help.

MORE TIPS

- Penmanship counts: not everyone has good penmanship, but in preparation for the exam, you should do as much as you can to improve yours. If you do not write legibly on your essays, you are jeopardizing your score. You cannot expect tired, overworked, AP readers to struggle with your essay needlessly. When you write your practice essays, always use blue or black ink and always write with an imagined reader in mind.

- This exam is about scholarship. You should think of yourself as you embark on this "quest" as an upper level scholar—a college student, really. If you wear the garb of scholar, even metaphorically, it will influence how you think about things.

- Your attitude is more important than you think—it influences everything, even your physical well-being. A positive attitude will give you energy and confidence. A negative attitude will
    - *limit your ability to read carefully (you'll want to rush, skim, get it over with)*
    - *lead to frustration and fatigue*
    - *keep you from having an open mind*
    - *possibly infect others, giving them doubt about their own abilities*

- You need to study hard and take the exam seriously, but also realize that it is just one test of what you know—at one point in your life. It is not the most important thing you will ever do. Try to keep it all in perspective.

PART II:
ELEMENTS OF LITERATURE AND MORE

Summary of Literary Periods, Concepts, and Authors

OVERVIEW

Literature might be thought of as the creative measure of history. Great writers, poets, and playwrights mold their sense of life and the events of their time (their own histories) into works of art. It seems impossible to disconnect most literary works from their historical context, but the themes that make their work universal and enduring perhaps do transcend time in that they speak to people of all time, ensuring us that we are all part of something much larger than simply the here and now.

When you look at the literary concepts below and study the timeline, you will see that shifts in literary theory or tradition are often precipitated by major events in history, most notably wars. The ways that history is linked to literature are endless, and this chapter only hints at some of them.

This chapter is not here for you to memorize. In fact there are rarely questions on the exam that expect you to know particular literary periods and their characteristics. However, it will not hurt you to have a sense of how literature (particularly Western literature) has evolved over time. And this timeline and the representative authors will help you determine a reading list for your study.

A FEW MAJOR CONCEPTS OR "ISMS"

The following list is given in chronological order.

Romanticism (mid-19th century)

- Valued feeling over reason
- Valued the individual, but recognized the alienation of the individual
- Literature characterized by elements of the supernatural, appreciation for the beauty of nature, personal introspection

Transcendentalism (mid-19th century)

- An offshoot of American Romanticism led by Bronson Alcott, Henry David Thoreau, and Ralph Waldo Emerson
- Favored self-reliance and non-conformism
- Sought to see the sublime in the ordinary
- Believed that to transcend was to reach beyond ordinary experience—self perfection was an aim

Realism (mid- to late 19th century)

- Pre– and post–Civil war
- Writers rejected sentimentality, wanted to represent true life experience, including the way people really acted and spoke
- Shunned flowery diction and romanticism
- The rise of the women's movement also significant

Regionalism (19th century)

- Extension of Realism
- Focus on local setting, customs, and dialects

Naturalism (19th century)

- Extension of Realism
- Themes are darker: crime, poverty, prejudice, etc.
- Naturalist writers tried to understand scientific or psychological reasons behind behavior

Imagism (early 20th century)

- Movement in poetry that favored the use of images as the things themselves
- Motto: "The natural object is always the adequate symbol."
- Willingness to play with forms
- Most notable poets: Ezra Pound and William Carlos Williams

The Lost Generation (1914–)

- The Lost Generation is the phrase coined by writer Gertrude Stein and later made popular by Ernest Hemingway
- Referred to the generation who lost fathers, husbands, sons and brothers in World War I and who felt aimless and without foundation
- Many of the lost were disillusioned by traditional American values and became expatriots, who chose to leave the United States for Europe, Mexico, and elsewhere. (Paris was an especially favored destination.)

The Harlem Renaissance (1920s)

- The explosion of African American visual art, dance, music, and literature in the 1920s, primarily centered in Harlem, New York
- Poet Langston Hughes is often seen as the symbol of the period.

Modernism (1918–1945)

- The prolific period between the end of World War I and the end of World War II
- Other historical context:
    - ▸ *The industrial revolution and the age of machines*
    - ▸ *Mass immigration to the United States*
    - ▸ *Women's rights (19ᵗʰ amendment)*
    - ▸ *The Great Depression*
- Alienation and the loss of the individual to the machine are major themes.

Post Modernism (1945–)

- Begins with detonation of atom bombs in Japan to end World War II
- Key markers:
    - ▸ *Post-apocalyptic themes*
    - ▸ *Satire*
    - ▸ *The absurd*
    - ▸ *Anti-heroes*
    - ▸ *The rise of multiculturalism and diverse voices*
- Themes:
    - ▸ *Alienation due to race, gender, and sexual orientation*
    - ▸ *Intolerance*
    - ▸ *Political and social oppression*

The Beat Movement (1950s)

- Led by poet Allen Ginsberg and novelist Jack Kerouac
- Rejected mainstream American values and embraced nonconformity and Eastern philosophy
- The forefather of the 1960s counter-culture movement (Hippie Movement)

Gonzo Journalism (1970–)

- Named by Hunter S. Thompson in 1970
- Refers to a new kind of journalism where the writer can be part of the story, blending fact and fiction

Magical Realism (1960's–)

- Magical or supernatural elements appear in otherwise realistic circumstances
- First considered an element of painting
- Mostly associated with Latin American writers, especially Gabriel Garcia Marquez, Carlos Fuentes, and Isabel Allende

Creative Nonfiction (late 20th and early 21st century)

- A genre that blends elements of literature with nonfiction
- Includes memoir, travel and place essays, personal narratives, etc.

LITERARY TIMELINE

Literary timelines are readily available to literature students. The value of a timeline is to show literary works in a historical context and in relationship to other works. The timeline below is not inclusive, but shows some of the major writers of each literary period. Consult Chapter 4 for lists of works cited on the AP Lit exam.

800–400 BCE

World Literature

Greek writers: Homer, *The Iliad* and *The Odyssey*

Sophocles, *Oedipus Rex* and *Antigone*

Euripedes, *Medea*

250 BCE–150 CE

World Literature

Roman writers: Vergil, *The Aeneid*

Horace, poet and satirist

Ovid, lyrical poet

450–1066

World Literature
Haiku poetry in Japan

British Literature (Anglo Saxon Period)
Beowulf

1066–1500

World Literature
Italian writers: Petrarch: sonnets

Dante Alighieri: *The Divine Comedy*

Boccaccio: *The Decameron*

British Literature (Middle English Period)
Geoffrey Chaucer: *Canterbury Tales*

German Johannes Gutenberg invents the printing press

1500–1660: The Renaissance

World Literature
Miguel de Cervantes, Spanish writer: *Don Quixote*

British Literature
Shakespeare

Christopher Marlow: *Dr. Faustus*

Ben Jonson, known for satirical plays and lyric poetry

John Donne, known for metaphysical conceits

Edmund Spenser: *The Faerie Queen*

Andrew Marvell: *To His Coy Mistress*

John Milton: *Paradise Lost*

1660–1785: The Neoclassical Period

World Literature
Molière, French, *Tartuffe*

Voltaire, French, *Candide*

Jean-Jacques Rousseau, French writer and philosopher

Johann Wolfgang von Goethe, German writer

British Literature

Alexander Pope, British poet

Daniel Defoe, *Robinson Crusoe* and *Moll Flanders*

Jonathan Swift: *Gulliver's Travels* and *A Modest Proposal*

Samuel Johnson

The rise of the novel

American Literature (Puritan/Colonial Period)

Jonathan Edwards, *Sinners in the Hands of an Angry God* (sermon)

Anne Bradstreet, poet

Puritan writing was God centered, plain in style, instructive in purpose.

1750–1800:

American Literature
(The Age of Reason/Revolutionary Literature)

Thomas Jefferson, Thomas Paine: *Common Sense*

Benjamin Franklin

African-American poet Phillis Wheatley, *Poetry on Various Subjects*

Period recognized by emerging nationalism; characterized by persuasive, philosophical writing: speeches, pamphlets, and the beginnings of newspapers in America.

1785–1830: The Romantic Period/Romanticism

British Literature

William Blake, William Wordsworth

Samuel Taylor Coleridge: *The Rime of the Ancient Mariner*

Jane Austen

Lord Byron

Percy Bysshe Shelley

John Keats

Alfred Lord Tennyson

Mary Shelley: *Frankenstein*

American Literature

Washington Irving: *Rip Van Winkle*

William Cullen Bryant: *Thanatopsis*

James Fenimore Cooper: *The Last of the Mohicans*

Nathaniel Hawthorne (often included in this period), see below.

1832–1901: The Victorian Period

World Literature

Henrik Ibsen, Norwegian dramatist: *A Doll's House*

Victor Hugo, French: *Les Misérables*

Gustave Flaubert, French: *Madame Bovary*

British Literature

Robert Browning, poet

Elizabeth Barrett Browning, poet

Charles Dickens: *Great Expectations*

Charlotte Brontë: *Jane Eyre*

Emily Brontë: *Wuthering Heights*

William Makepeace Thackeray: *Vanity Fair*

George Eliot, a.k.a. Marian Evans: *Middlemarch*

American Literature

Henry James

Frederick Douglass: *Narrative of the Life of Frederick Douglass, an American Slave*

Harriet Jacobs: *Incidents in the Life of a Slave Girl*

Paul Laurence Dunbar: *Lyrics of a Lowly Life*

1840–1860: American Renaissance

Transcendentalism and American Gothic (dark romantics)

Emily Dickinson, poet

Walt Whitman: *Leaves of Grass*

Nathaniel Hawthorne: *The Scarlet Letter*

Herman Melville: *Moby Dick*

Edgar Allan Poe, poems and short stories

Transcendentalist Writers

Ralph Waldo Emerson, essays and aphorisms

Henry David Thoreau: *Walden*

Bronson Alcott

Margaret Fuller, first major feminist writer

1855–1900: American Realism/Regionalism

Mark Twain (born Samuel Clemens): *The Adventures of Huckleberry Finn*

Bret Harte: regional writer

Stephen Crane: *The Red Badge of Courage*

Kate Chopin: *The Awakening*

Charlotte Perkins Gilman: *The Yellow Wallpaper*

1901–1914

British (Edwardian Period)

Joseph Conrad, Polish/British author: *Heart of Darkness*

American (Naturalism)

Theodore Dreiser, novelist: *Sister Carrie* (1990)

W.E.B. Du Bois, sociologist and author: *The Souls of Black Folk*

Jack London, novelist: *The Call of the Wild*

Edith Wharton, novelist: *Ethan Frome*

1919–1945

Modernism

World Literature

Albert Camus, French writer: *The Stranger*

British Literature

George Orwell (born Eric Blair): *Animal Farm* and *1984*

American Literature

John Steinbeck, Nobel Prize novelist: *Of Mice and Men* and *The Grapes of Wrath*

Zora Neale Hurston, novelist: *Their Eyes Were Watching God*

Langston Hughes, poet

Tennessee Williams, playwright: *The Glass Menagerie*

1950– : Post Modernism

British Literature

William Golding, British author: *Lord of the Flies*

American Literature

(Note: Ethnicities are listed below only to show the range of diversity in literature in this period.)

J.D.Salinger, novelist: *The Catcher in the Rye*

Ralph Ellison, African American novelist: *Invisible Man*

Arthur Miller, playwright: *The Crucible* and *Death of a Salesman*

Ray Bradbury, science fiction writer: *Fahrenheit 451*

Eugene O'Neill, playwright: *Long Day's Journey Into Night*

Jack Kerouac, Beat writer: *On the Road*

Elie Wiesel, Romanian-American writer: *Night*

Joseph Heller, novelist: *Catch 22* (1961)

John Knowles, novelist: *A Separate Peace*

Ken Kesey, American author: *One Flew Over the Cuckoo's Nest*

Sylvia Plath, known mostly for poetry (1932-63): *The Bell Jar* (1963)

Chaim Potok, Jewish-American novelist: *The Chosen*

Maya Angelou, African-American author: *I Know Why the Caged Bird Sings*

Toni Morrison, African-American Nobel Prize novelist: *The Bluest Eye*

Rudolfo Anaya, Mexican-American writer: *Bless Me, Ultima*

Maxine Hong Kingston, Asian-American writer: *The Woman Warrior*

Alice Walker, African-American writer: *The Color Purple*

August Wilson, African-American, Pulitzer Prize winning playwright: *Fences* and *The Piano Lesson*

Sandra Cisneros, Hispanic-American writer: *The House on Mango Street*

Louise Erdrich, Native American writer: *Love Medicine*

Amy Tan, Asian-American novelist: *The Joy Luck Club*

FEATURED AUTHORS

This list below is from the *2008 Course Description* as published by the College Board. The purpose of this list is to suggest the broad range of authors that can be considered for study in an AP Lit course. Use this list in combination with the timeline above and the list of literary works in Chapter 4 to create a reading list for yourself. Remember, it is far better to know five or six works in depth, than to have a cursory knowledge of more.

POETRY

W. H. Auden; Elizabeth Bishop; William Blake; Anne Bradstreet; Edward Kamau Brathwaite; Gwendolyn Brooks; Robert Browning; George Gordon, Lord Byron; Lorna Dee Cervantes; Geoffrey Chaucer; Lucille Clifton; Samuel Taylor Coleridge; Billy Collins; H. D. (Hilda Doolittle); Emily Dickinson; John Donne; Rita Dove; Paul Laurence Dunbar; T. S. Eliot; Robert Frost; Joy Harjo; Seamus Heaney; George Herbert; Garrett Hongo; Gerard Manley Hopkins; Langston Hughes; Ben Jonson; John Keats; Philip Larkin; Robert Lowell; Andrew Marvell; John Milton; Marianne Moore; Sylvia Plath; Edgar Allan Poe; Alexander Pope; Adrienne Rich; Anne Sexton; William Shakespeare; Percy Bysshe Shelley; Leslie Marmon Silko; Cathy Song; Wallace Stevens; Alfred, Lord Tennyson; Derek Walcott; Walt Whitman; Richard Wilbur; William Carlos Williams; William Wordsworth; William Butler Yeats

DRAMA

Aeschylus; Edward Albee; Amiri Baraka; Samuel Beckett; Anton Chekhov; Caryl Churchill; William Congreve; Athol Fugard; Lorraine Hansberry; Lillian Hellman; David Henry Hwang; Henrik Ibsen; Ben Jonson; David Mamet; Arthur Miller; Molière; Marsha Norman; Sean O'Casey; Eugene O'Neill; Suzan-Lori Parks; Harold Pinter; Luigi Pirandello; William Shakespeare; George Bernard Shaw; Sam Shepard; Sophocles; Tom Stoppard; Luis Valdez; Oscar Wilde; Tennessee Williams; August Wilson

FICTION (NOVEL AND SHORT STORY)

Chinua Achebe; Sherman Alexie; Isabel Allende; Rudolfo Anaya; Margaret Atwood; Jane Austen; James Baldwin; Saul Bellow; Charlotte Brontë; Emily Brontë; Raymond Carver; Willa Cather; Sandra Cisneros; John Cheever; Kate Chopin; Joseph Conrad; Edwidge Danticat; Daniel Defoe; Anita Desai; Charles Dickens; Fyodor Dostoevsky; George Eliot; Ralph Ellison; Louise Erdrich; William Faulkner; Henry Fielding; F. Scott Fitzgerald; E. M. Forster; Thomas Hardy; Nathaniel Hawthorne; Ernest Hemingway; Zora Neale Hurston; Kazuo Ishiguro; Henry James; Ha Jin; Edward P. Jones; James

Joyce; Maxine Hong Kingston; Joy Kogawa; Jhumpa Lahiri; Margaret Laurence; D. H. Lawrence; Chang-rae Lee; Bernard Malamud; Gabriel García Márquez; Cormac McCarthy; Ian McEwan; Herman Melville; Toni Morrison; Bharati Mukherjee; Vladimir Nabokov; Flannery O'Connor; Orhan Pamuk; Katherine Anne Porter; Marilynne Robinson; Jonathan Swift; Mark Twain; John Updike; Alice Walker; Evelyn Waugh; Eudora Welty; Edith Wharton; John Edgar Wideman; Virginia Woolf; Richard Wright

EXPOSITORY PROSE

Joseph Addison; Gloria Anzaldúa; Matthew Arnold; James Baldwin; James Boswell; Jesús Colón; Joan Didion; Frederick Douglass; W.E.B. Du Bois; Ralph Waldo Emerson; William Hazlitt; bell hooks; Samuel Johnson; Charles Lamb; Thomas Macaulay; Mary McCarthy; John Stuart Mill; George Orwell; Michael Pollan; Richard Rodriguez; Edward Said; Lewis Thomas; Henry David Thoreau; E. B. White; Virginia Woolf

Summary of Literary Texts

OVERVIEW

The purpose of this chapter is to acquaint you with the variety and types of literary works that have been on past exams and may appear on future exams. While you are not expected to have read all of these works—that would be impossible—you are expected to have read a wide variety of works. It is better to know *five to seven* novels/plays very well than to have a cursory knowledge of more literary works.

If you study the first list below, you will find that most of the titles are novels or plays. Some short fictional works are listed along with a few (very few) non-fiction texts.

If time is short, focus on reading and studying a few novels and plays. Choose those most often cited on the AP Lit exam if you have no other impulse guiding your decision. See the list below.

Also, if you look at the tags for the most prominently cited works, you'll see some common denominators, which may indicate the types of themes the College Board tends to favor in its selection of texts for the exam. Common themes include:

- a heroic journey or quest
- self determination or self discovery
- coming of age or maturity (bildungsroman)
- awakenings or epiphanies: individual, spiritual, etc.
- disparity and oppression: class, economy, race, sex, etc.

In general, the AP Lit exam is going to present obscure texts in the multiple-choice section, presumably so that a greater percentage of students will be unfamiliar with them. Therefore, you cannot expect to study and know those passages and poems ahead of time. Instead, your success hinges on your careful reading and analysis of these passages and poems on test day.

No doubt you have already read some of the works listed in this chapter. To aid you in remembering the key concepts for those works, there is a graphic organizer presented at the end of this chapter called *Remembering Major Works*. This organizer is not meant to represent everything you might need to know about a certain text, but it gives you a concise format for recording a good summary of major novels or plays. It is meant to be a memory tool.

If you have read very few books at this point, use the *Key Concepts* section below to find books that you would enjoy reading and studying. Be sure to choose a variety, not all 18th century British novels, for example. It is good to read old and new, American and British, fiction and drama. The key is to mix it up.

TEXTS OF LITERARY MERIT

The third essay question on the AP Lit exam is open-ended. You are given a general prompt and expected to apply that prompt to a literary work with which you are thoroughly familiar. I cannot impress upon you enough the importance of choosing a novel or a play of literary merit. If you do not, you risk a poor score.

You may believe that *Harry Potter and the Prisoner of Azkaban*, *Breaking Dawn*, or even *Green Eggs and Ham* is the most profound book you have ever read and you might even believe that it perfectly fits the prompt, but—and this is very important—if you choose such a book, you are taking a big risk. Not only will you have to argue your thesis, but you will also need to argue that the text you have chosen is of enduring literary quality. On the AP Lit exam you don't have time for such an argument!

Not only that, the College Board is also testing your ability to read and understand a complex text. While a great young adult novel might be engaging, it is probably not that complex. Choose your text wisely. You might want to save yourself time and possible grief by choosing five to seven novels or plays from the list that follows.

TITLES CITED IN THE FREE-RESPONSE ESSAYS SINCE 1973

(This list originated with Norma J. Wilkerson and is kept up-to-date by Sandra Effinger.)

The following alphabetical list shows the specific years the titles were referred to on the AP Lit exam. Specific years are in parentheses; titles of novels and plays are in italics; and titles of long/epic poems are set off by quotation marks.

A

Absalom, Absalom by William Faulkner (76, 00)

Adam Bede by George Eliot (06)

The Adventures of Huckleberry Finn by Mark Twain (80, 82, 85, 91, 92, 94, 95, 96, 99, 05, 06, 07, 08)

The Aeneid by Vergil (06)

Agnes of God by John Pielmeier (00)

The Age of Innocence by Edith Wharton (97, 02, 03, 08)

Alias Grace by Margaret Atwood (00, 04, 08)

All the King's Men by Robert Penn Warren (00, 02, 04, 07, 08)

All My Sons by Arthur Miller (85, 90)

All the Pretty Horses by Cormac McCarthy (95, 96, 06, 07, 08)

America is in the Heart by Carlos Bulosan (95)

An American Tragedy by Theodore Dreiser (81, 82, 95, 03)

The American by Henry James (05)

Anna Karenina by Leo Tolstoy (80, 91, 99, 03, 04, 06, 08)

Another Country by James Baldwin (95)

Antigone by Sophocles (79, 80, 90, 94, 99, 03, 05)

Anthony and Cleopatra by William Shakespeare (80, 91)

Apprenticeship of Duddy Kravitz by Mordecai Richler (94)

Armies of the Night by Norman Mailer (76)

As I Lay Dying by William Faulkner (78, 89, 90, 94, 01, 04, 06, 07)

As You Like It by William Shakespeare (92, 05. 06)

Atonement by Ian McEwan (07)

Autobiography of an Ex-Colored Man by James Weldon Johnson (02, 05)

The Awakening by Kate Chopin (87, 88, 91, 92, 95, 97, 99, 02, 07)

B

"The Bear" by William Faulkner (94. 06)

Beloved by Toni Morrison (90, 99, 01, 03, 05, 07)

A Bend in the River by V. S. Naipaul (03)

Benito Cereno by Herman Melville (89)

Billy Budd by Herman Melville (79, 81, 82, 83, 85, 99, 02, 04, 05, 07, 08)

The Birthday Party by Harold Pinter (89, 97)

Black Boy by Richard Wright (06, 08)

Bleak House by Charles Dickens (94, 00, 04)

Bless Me, Ultima by Rudolfo Anaya (94, 96, 97, 99, 04, 05, 06, 08)

The Blind Assassin by Margaret Atwood (07)

The Bluest Eye by Toni Morrison (95, 08)

Bone: A Novel by Fae M. Ng (03)

The Bonesetter's Daughter by Amy Tan (06, 07)

Brave New World by Aldous Huxley (89, 05)

Brighton Rock by Graham Greene (79)

The Brothers Karamazov by Fyodor Dostoevsky (90, 08)

C

Candida by George Bernard Shaw (80)

Candide by Voltaire (80, 86, 87, 91, 95, 96, 04, 06)

The Canterbury Tales by Geoffrey Chaucer (06)

The Caretaker by Harold Pinter (85)

Catch-22 by Joseph Heller (82, 85, 87, 89, 94, 01, 03, 04, 05, 07, 08)

The Catcher in the Rye by J. D. Salinger (01, 08)

Cat on a Hot Tin Roof by Tennessee Williams (00)

Cat's Eye by Margaret Atwood (94, 08)

The Centaur by John Updike (81)

Ceremony by Leslie Marmon Silko (94, 96, 97, 99, 01, 03, 05, 06, 07)

The Cherry Orchard by Anton Chekhov (77, 06, 07)

The Chosen by Chaim Potok (08)

"Civil Disobedience" by Henry David Thoreau (76)

Cold Mountain by Charles Frazier (06, 08)

The Color Purple by Alice Walker (92, 94, 95, 96, 97, 05, 08)

Coming Through Slaughter by Michael Ondaatje (01)

Cry, The Beloved Country by Alan Paton (85, 87, 91, 95, 96, 07)

Crime and Punishment by Fyodor Dostoevsky (76, 79, 80, 82, 88, 96, 99, 00, 01, 02, 03, 04, 05)

"The Crisis" by Thomas Paine (76)

The Crucible by Arthur Miller (83, 86, 89, 04, 05)

D

Daisy Miller by Henry James (97, 03)

Dancing at Lughnasa by Brian Friel (01)

David Copperfield by Charles Dickens (78, 83, 06)

"The Dead" by James Joyce (97)

The Death of Ivan Ilyich by Leo Tolstoy (86)

Death of a Salesman by Arthur Miller (86, 88, 94, 03, 04, 05, 07)

Delta Wedding by Eudora Welty (97)

Desire under the Elms by Eugene O'Neill (81)

Dinner at the Homesick Restaurant by Anne Tyler (97)

The Divine Comedy by Dante Alighieri (06)

The Diviners by Margaret Laurence (95)

Doctor Faustus by Christopher Marlowe (79, 86, 99, 04)

A Doll's House by Henrik Ibsen (83, 87, 88, 95, 05)

The Dollmaker by Harriet Arnot (91)

Don Quixote by Miguel de Cervantes (01, 04, 06, 08)

Dreaming in Cuban by Cristina Garcia (03)

Dutchman by Amiri Baraka/Leroi Jones (03, 06)

E

East of Eden by John Steinbeck (06)

Emma by Jane Austen (96, 08)

An Enemy of the People by Henrik Ibsen (76, 80, 87, 99, 01, 07)

Equus by Peter Shaffer (92, 99, 00, 01, 08)

Ethan Frome by Edith Wharton (80, 85, 03, 05, 06, 07)

The Eumenides by Aeschylus (in *The Orestia*) (96)

F

The Fall by Albert Camus (81)

A Farewell to Arms by Ernest Hemingway (99, 04)

The Father by August Strindberg (01)

Fathers and Sons by Ivan Turgenev (90)

Faust by Johann Goethe (02)

The Federalist by Alexander Hamilton (76)

Fences by August Wilson (02, 05)

Fifth Business by Robertson Davis (00)

A Fine Balance by Rohinton Mistry (03, 07)

The Fixer by Bernard Malamud (07)

For Whom the Bell Tolls by Ernest Hemingway (03, 06)

Frankenstein by Mary Shelley (89, 00, 03, 06, 08)

G

A Gathering of Old Men by Ernest Gaines (00)

A Gesture Life by Chang-Rae Lee (04, 05)

Ghosts by Henrik Ibsen (00, 04)

The Glass Menagerie by Tennessee Williams (90, 94, 97, 99, 02, 08)

Going After Cacciato by Tim O'Brien (01, 06)

The Good Soldier by Ford Maddox Ford (00)

The Grapes of Wrath by John Steinbeck (95, 03, 06)

Great Expectations by Charles Dickens (79, 80, 88, 89, 92, 95, 96, 00, 01, 02, 03, 04, 05, 07, 08)

The Great Gatsby by F. Scott Fitzgerald (82, 83, 88, 91, 92, 97, 00, 02, 04, 05, 07)

Go Tell It on the Mountain by James Baldwin (83, 88, 90, 05)

Gulliver's Travels by Jonathan Swift (87, 89, 01, 04, 06)

H

The Hairy Ape by Eugene O'Neill (89)

Hamlet by William Shakespeare (88, 94, 97, 99, 00)

The Handmaid's Tale by Margaret Atwood (03)

Hard Times by Charles Dickens (87, 90)

Heart of Darkness by Joseph Conrad (76, 91, 94, 96, 99, 00, 01, 02, 03, 04, 06)

The Heart of the Matter by Graham Greene (71)

Hedda Gabler by Henrik Ibsen (79, 92, 00, 02, 03, 05)

Henry IV, Parts I and II by William Shakespeare (80, 90, 08)

Henry V by William Shakespeare (02)

A High Wind in Jamaica by Richard Hughes (08)

The Homecoming by Harold Pinter (78, 90)

House Made of Dawn by N. Scott Momaday (95, 06)

The House of Mirth by Edith Wharton (04, 07)

The House of Seven Gables by Nathaniel Hawthorne (89)

The House on Mango Street by Sandra Cisneros (08)

I

The Iliad by Homer (80)

The Importance of Being Earnest by Oscar Wilde (06)

In the Lake of the Woods by Tim O'Brien (00)

In the Time of Butterflies by Julia Alvarez (05)

Invisible Man by Ralph Ellison (76, 77, 78, 82, 83, 85, 86, 87, 88, 89, 91, 94, 95, 96, 97, 01, 03, 04, 05, 07, 08)

J

Jane Eyre by Charlotte Brontë (78, 79, 80, 88, 91, 94, 95, 96, 97, 99, 00, 05, 07, 08)

Jasmine by Bharati Mukherjee (99)

J.B. by Archibald MacLeish (81, 94)

Joe Turner's Come and Gone by August Wilson (00)

The Joy Luck Club by Amy Tan (97, 03)

Joseph Andrews by Henry Fielding (99)

Jude the Obscure by Thomas Hardy (76, 80, 85, 87, 95)

Julius Caesar by William Shakespeare (82, 97, 07)

The Jungle by Upton Sinclair (77, 78, 82, 88, 89, 90, 96)

K

Kafka on the Shore by Haruki Murakami (08)

King Lear by William Shakespeare (77, 78, 82, 88, 89, 90, 96, 01, 03, 06, 08)

The Kite Runner by Khaled Hosseini (07, 08)

L

A Lesson before Dying by Ernest Gaines (99)

Letters from an American Farmer by de Crèvecoeur (76)

Light in August by William Faulkner (79, 81, 82, 83, 85, 95, 99, 03, 06)

The Little Foxes by Lillian Hellman (85, 90)

Little Women by Louisa May Alcott (08)

Long Day's Journey into Night by Eugene O'Neill (90, 03, 07)

Lord Jim by Joseph Conrad (77, 78, 82, 86, 00, 03, 07)

Lord of the Flies by William Golding (85, 08)

The Loved One by Evelyn Waugh (89)

Love Medicine by Louise Erdrich (95)

"Love Song of J. Alfred Prufrock" by T. S. Eliot (85)

Lysistrata by Aristophanes (87)

M

Macbeth by William Shakespeare (83, 99, 03, 05)

Madame Bovary by Gustave Flaubert (80, 85, 04, 05, 06)

Main Street by Sinclair Lewis (87)

Major Barbara by George Bernard Shaw (79, 96, 04, 07)

Man and Superman by George Bernard Shaw (81)

Mansfield Park by Jane Austen (03, 06)

Master Harold...and the Boys by Athol Fugard (03, 08)

The Mayor of Casterbridge by Thomas Hardy (94, 99, 00, 02, 07)

M. Butterfly by David Henry Wang (95)

Medea by Euripides (82, 92, 95, 01, 03)

The Member of the Wedding by Carson McCullers (97, 08)

The Merchant of Venice by William Shakespeare (85, 91, 95, 02, 03)

Metamorphosis by Franz Kafka (78, 89)

Middlemarch by George Eliot (95, 04, 05, 07)

Middle Passage by V. S. Naipaul (06)

A Midsummer Night's Dream by William Shakespeare (06)

The Mill on the Floss by George Eliot (90, 92, 04)

The Misanthrope by Molière (2008)

Miss Lonelyhearts by Nathanael West (89)

Moby Dick by Herman Melville (76, 77, 78, 79, 80, 89, 94, 96, 01, 03, 04, 05, 06, 07)

Moll Flanders by Daniel Defoe (76, 77, 86, 87, 95)

Monkey Bridge by Lan Cao (00, 03)

The Moor's Last Sigh by Salman Rushdie (07)

Mother Courage and Her Children by Berthold Brecht (85, 87, 06)

Mrs. Dalloway by Virginia Woolf (94, 97, 04, 05, 07)

Mrs. Warren's Profession by George Bernard Shaw (87, 90, 95, 02)

Much Ado About Nothing by William Shakespeare (97)

Murder in the Cathedral by T. S. Eliot (76, 80, 85, 95, 07)

"My Last Duchess" by Robert Browning (85)

My Antonia by Willa Cather (03, 08)

My Name is Asher Lev by Chaim Potok (03)

N

Native Son by Richard Wright (79, 82, 85, 87, 95, 01, 04)

Native Speaker by Chang-Rae Lee (99, 03, 07, 08)

1984 by George Orwell (87, 94)

No Exit by John Paul Sartre (86)

No-No Boy by John Okada (95)

Notes from the Underground by Fyodor Dostoevsky (89)

O

Obasan by Joy Kogawa (94, 95, 04, 05, 06, 07)

The Odyssey by Homer (86, 06)

Oedipus Rex by Sophocles (77, 85, 88, 00, 03, 04)

Of Mice and Men by John Steinbeck (01)

Old School by Tobias Wolff (08)

One Day in the Life of Ivan Denisovich by Alexander
  Solzhenitsyn (05)

One Hundred Years of Solitude by Gabriel Garcia Marquez (89,
  04)

One Flew Over the Cuckoo's Nest by Ken Kesey (01)

O Pioneers! by Willa Cather (06)

The Optimist's Daughter by D. H. Lawrence (94)

The Orestia by Aeschylus (90)

Orlando: A Biography by Virginia Woolf (04)

Othello by William Shakespeare (79, 85, 88, 92, 95, 03, 04, 07)

Our Mutual Friend by Charles Dickens (90)

Our Town by Thornton Wilder (86, 97)

Out of Africa by Isaak Dinesen (06)

P

Pale Fire by Vladimir Nabokov (01)

Pamela by Samuel Richardson (86)

A Passage to India by E. M. Forster (77, 78, 88, 91, 92, 07)

Paradise Lost by John Milton (85, 86)

Peer Gynt by Henrik Ibsen (06)

Père Goriot by Honoré de Balzac (02)

Persuasion by Jane Austen (90, 05, 07)

Phaedre by Jean Racine (92, 03)

The Piano Lesson by August Wilson (96, 99, 07, 08)

The Picture of Dorian Gray by Oscar Wilde (02)

The Plague by Albert Camus (02)

Pnin by Vladimir Nabokov (97)

Pocho by Jose Antonio Villareal (02, 08)

Portrait of a Lady by Henry James (88, 92, 96, 03, 05, 07)

Portrait of the Artist as a Young Man by James Joyce (76, 77, 80, 86, 88, 96, 99, 04, 05, 08)

The Power and the Glory by Graham Greene (95)

Praisesong for the Widow by Paule Marshall (96)

Pride and Prejudice by Jane Austen (83, 88, 92, 97, 08)

The Prime of Miss Jean Brodie by Muriel Spark (90, 08)

Push by Sapphire (07)

Pygmalion by George Bernard Shaw (03, 05, 08)

R

Ragtime by E. L. Doctorow (03, 07)

A Raisin in the Sun by Lorraine Hansberry (87, 90, 94, 96, 99, 07)

The Rape of the Lock by Alexander Pope (81)

The Red Badge of Courage by Stephen Crane (08)

Redburn by Herman Melville (87)

The Remains of the Day by Kazuo Ishiguro (00, 03)

Reservation Blues by Sherman Alexie (08)

The Return of the Native by Thomas Hardy (07)

Richard III by William Shakespeare (79)

A River Runs Through It by Norman Maclean (08)

A Room of One's Own by Virginia Woolf (76)

A Room with a View by E. M. Forster (03)

Romeo and Juliet by William Shakespeare (90, 92, 97, 08)

Rosencrantz and Guildenstern Are Dead by Tom Stoppard (81, 94, 00, 04, 05, 06)

S

Saint Joan by George Bernard Shaw (95)

The Scarlet Letter by Nathaniel Hawthorne (77, 78, 83, 88, 91, 99, 02, 04, 05, 06)

Sent for You Yesterday by John E. Wideman (03)

A Separate Peace by John Knowles (82, 07)

The Shipping News by E. Annie Proulx (97)

Silas Marner by George Eliot (02)

Sister Carrie by Theodore Dreiser (87, 02, 04)

Slaughterhouse Five by Kurt Vonnegut (91, 04)

Snow Falling on Cedars by David Guterson (00)

Song of Solomon by Toni Morrison (81, 88, 96, 00, 04, 05, 06, 07)

Sons and Lovers by D. H. Lawrence (77, 90)

The Sound and the Fury by William Faulkner (77, 86, 97, 01, 07, 08)

The Stone Angel by Margaret Laurence (96, 04)

The Stranger by Albert Camus (79, 82, 86, 04)

A Streetcar Named Desire by Tennessee Williams (91, 92, 01, 04, 07, 08)

The Street by Ann Petry (07)

Sula by Toni Morrison (92, 97, 02, 04, 07, 08)

Surfacing by Margaret Atwood (05)

The Sun Also Rises by Ernest Hemingway (85, 91, 95, 96, 04, 05)

T

A Tale of Two Cities by Charles Dickens (82, 91, 04, 08)

Tarftuffe by Molière (87)

The Tempest by William Shakespeare (78, 96, 03, 05, 07)

Tess of the D'Urbervilles by Thomas Hardy (82, 91, 03, 06, 07)

Their Eyes Were Watching God by Zora Neale Hurston (88, 90, 91, 96. 04, 05, 06, 07, 08)

Things Fall Apart by Chinua Achebe (91, 97, 03)

The Things They Carried by Tim O'Brien (04)

A Thousand Acres by Jane Smiley (06)

To Kill a Mockingbird by Harper Lee (08)

To the Lighthouse by Virginia Woolf (77, 86, 88, 08)

Tom Jones by Henry Fielding (90, 00, 06, 08)

The Trial by Franz Kafka (88, 89, 00)

Trifles by Susan Glaspell (00)

Tristram Shandy by Laurence Sterne (86)

The Turn of the Screw by Henry James (92, 94, 00, 02, 04, 08)

Twelfth Night by William Shakespeare (85, 94, 96)

Typical American by Gish Jen (02, 03, 05)

U

Uncle Tom's Cabin by Harriet Beecher Stowe (87)

V

The Vicar of Wakefield by Oliver Goldsmith (06)

Victory by Joseph Conrad (83)

Volpone by Ben Jonson (83)

W

Waiting for Godot by Samuel Beckett (77, 85, 86, 89, 94, 01)

The Warden by Anthony Trollope (96)

Washington Square by Henry James (90)

The Wasteland by T. S. Eliot (81)

Watch on the Rhine by Lillian Hellman (87)

The Way We Live Now by Anthony Trollope (06)

We Were the Mulvaneys by Joyce Carol Oates (07)

Who's Afraid of Virginia Woolf? by Edward Albee (88, 94, 00, 04, 07)

Wide Sargasso Sea by Jean Rhys (89, 92, 05, 07, 08)

The Wild Duck by Henrik Ibsen (78)

Winter in the Blood by James Welch (95)

Winter's Tale by William Shakespeare (82, 89, 95, 06)

Wise Blood by Flannery O'Connor (82, 89, 95)

Woman Warrior by Maxine Hong Kingston (91, 08)

Wuthering Heights by Emily Brontë (77, 78, 79, 83, 86, 88, 89, 90, 91, 92, 96, 97, 99, 01, 06, 07, 08)

Z

The Zoo Story by Edward Albee (82, 01)

Zoot Suit by Luis Valdez (95)

MOST FREQUENTLY CITED WORKS (1970–2008)

(This list was also compiled by Sandra Effinger.)

Frequency of Appearance	Title, author
22	*Invisible Man* by Ralph Ellison
18	*Wuthering Heights* by Emily Brontë
15	*Great Expectations* by Charles Dickens *Jane Eyre* by Charlotte Brontë *Moby Dick* by Herman Melville
14	*Crime and Punishment* by Fyodor Dostoevsky
13	*The Adventures of Huckleberry Finn* by Mark Twain *Heart of Darkness* by Joseph Conrad *King Lear* by William Shakespeare
11	*Billy Budd* by Herman Melville *Catch-22* by Joseph Heller *The Scarlet Letter* by Nathaniel Hawthorne *The Great Gatsby* by F. Scott Fitzgerald *Portrait of the Artist as a Young Man* by James Joyce
10	*The Awakening* by Kate Chopin *Light in August* by William Faulkner *Ceremony* by Leslie Marmon Silko
9	*As I Lay Dying* by William Faulkner *Their Eyes Were Watching God* by Zora Neale Hurston

Frequency of Appearance	Title, author
8	*Anna Karenina* by Leo Tolstoy *Antigone* by Sophocles *Bless Me, Ultima* by Rudolfo Anaya *Candide* by Voltaire *The Glass Menagerie* by Tennessee Williams *The Jungle* by Upton Sinclair *Native Son* by Richard Wright *Othello* by William Shakespeare *Song of Solomon* by Toni Morrison
7	*Beloved* by Toni Morrison *The Color Purple* by Alice Walker *The Crucible* by Arthur Miller *Cry, The Beloved Country* by Alan Paton *Death of a Salesman* by Arthur Miller *Lord Jim* by Joseph Conrad *A Passage to India* by E. M. Forster *A Raisin in the Sun* by Lorraine Hansberry *A Streetcar Named Desire* by Tennessee Williams *Waiting for Godot* by Samuel Beckett
6	*A Doll's House* by Henrik Ibsen *An Enemy of the People* by Henrik Ibsen *Ethan Frome* by Edith Wharton *Gulliver's Travels* by Jonathan Swift *Hedda Gabler* by Henrik Ibsen *Jude the Obscure* by Thomas Hardy *Madame Bovary* by Gustave Flaubert *Moll Flanders* by Daniel Defoe *Obasan* by Joy Kogawa *Portrait of a Lady* by Henry James *Rosencrantz and Guildenstern Are Dead* by Tom Stoppard *The Sound and the Fury* by William Faulkner *The Sun Also Rises* by Ernest Hemingway *The Tempest* by William Shakespeare

Continued ➡

(Continued from previous page)

Frequency of Appearance	Title, author
5	*All the King's Men* by Robert Penn Warren *All the Pretty Horses* by Cormac McCarthy *Frankenstein* by Mary Shelley *Go Tell It on the Mountain* by James Baldwin *Hamlet* by William Shakespeare *The Mayor of Casterbridge* by Thomas Hardy *Medea* by Euripides *The Merchant of Venice* by William Shakespeare *Mrs. Warren's Profession* by George Bernard Shaw *Mrs. Dalloway* by Virginia Woolf *Murder in the Cathedral* by T. S. Eliot *Pride and Prejudice* by Jane Austen *Sula* by Toni Morrison *Tess of the D'Urbervilles* by Thomas Hardy *The Turn of the Screw* by Henry James *Who's Afraid of Virginia Woolf?* by Edward Albee *Wide Sargasso Sea* by Jean Rhys

KEY DETAILS FOR THE MOST FREQUENTLY CITED WORKS

The works listed below are shown in the same order as in the previous table, which means the titles at the top of the table are the most frequently cited works.

The purpose of this chart is not to supplant your reading, but merely to give you a brief glimpse of these works so you may choose several to read. It is important to your success on the exam that you be familiar with several works from these lists. The tags below give you an idea of themes and key literary elements for the work. Remember that you should read widely, which means old and new works of British, American, and world literature.

For more detailed summaries and descriptions, consult a variety of Internet study guides.

Invisible Man by Ralph Ellison, published 1952	**Genre:** novel (modern) **Setting:** 1930s, American South, New York (Harlem) **Main character:** narrator is unnamed black man **Main Plot/Idea/Concept:** search for self vs. the oppression of racism **Tags:** blindness, racism, symbolism
Wuthering Heights by Emily Brontë, published 1847	**Genre:** novel (gothic) **Setting:** 1700's, Yorkshire England **Main characters:** Mr. Lockwood (narrator), Nellie, Heathcliff, Catherine **Main Plot/Idea/Concept:** Catherine is caught between her love for Heathcliff and her desire to be a gentlewoman, but she decides to marry the genteel Edgar Linton. **Tags:** social class, love, revenge
Great Expectations by Charles Dickens, serialized from December 1860 to August 1861	**Genre:** novel (coming of age) **Setting:** Kent and London, England, mid-19th century **Main characters:** Pip, Joe, Mrs. Joe, Estella, Miss Havisham, Magwitch **Main Plot/Idea/Concept:** A poor young boy finds himself the recipient of some money from an unknown benefactor and he seeks to improve his status in life. **Tags:** love, ambition, self-improvement, social class, symbolism, foreshadowing
Jane Eyre by Charlotte Brontë, published 1847	**Genre:** novel, (Gothic and romantic) English **Setting:** early 19th century, England **Main characters:** Jane Eyre, Mr. Rochester **Main Plot/Idea/Concept:** Jane Eyre, as an adult, tells the story of her young life so far, from an orphan to a love-torn woman. **Tags:** love, self determination, social class, religion

Continued →

(Continued from previous page)

Moby Dick by Herman Melville, published 1851	**Genre:** novel **Setting:** 1830s or 1840s, aboard the whaling ship *The Pequod*, upon the Pacific, Atlantic, and Indian Oceans **Main characters:** Ishmael (narrator), Captain Ahab, Moby Dick (the white whale) **Main Plot/Idea/Concept:** Defying all odds, Captain Ahab commits his crew to hunting down and destroying Moby Dick because he sees him as representing all that is evil. **Tags:** epic adventure, allegory, quest, hubris
The Adventures of Huckleberry Finn by Mark Twain, published 1884	**Genre:** episodic/picaresque novel **Setting:** Mississippi River mid 1800s **Main characters:** Huckleberry Finn, Jim, Tom Sawyer, Miss Watson **Main Plot/Idea/Concept:** Huck, abused by his alcoholic father, escapes with a runaway slave named Jim. He struggles with whether or not to turn Jim in to the authorities. **Tags:** satire, American themes/setting, slavery, pragmatism vs. romanticism, dialect
Crime and Punishment by Fyodor Dostoevsky, 1866-1867	**Genre:** novel **Setting:** St. Petersburg, Russia and a Siberian prison **Main characters:** Raskolnikov, Luzhin, Porfiry Petrovich, Svidrigailov, Raskolnikov's conscience **Main Plot/Idea/Concept:** Raskolnikov is a poor ex-student who conceives of and carries out his plan to kill an unscrupulous pawnbroker for her money. He will gain wealth and rid the world of a horrible person. Raskolnikov attempts to convince himself that murder is acceptable if it achieves a higher purpose. **Tags:** psychology of crime and punishment, poverty, alienation from society, religious redemption, moral dilemma

King Lear by William Shakespeare, first folio 1623	**Genre:** play, tragedy **Setting:** England, 8th century BCE **Main characters:** King Lear of Britain; Lear's daughters Goneril, Regan, and Cordelia; Edmund, the bastard son of Gloucester **Main Plot/Idea/Concept:** King Lear decides to step down from his throne and divide his kingdom among his three daughters, but before doing so, he tests their loyalty. Goneril and Regan betray their father. **Tags:** madness, justice, authority versus chaos, betrayal, reconciliation, love and forgiveness, redemption, weather as a symbol
Heart of Darkness by Joseph Conrad, 1899 (serialized), 1902	**Genre:** short novel, novella **Setting:** late 19th century, primarily the Belgian Congo **Main characters:** Marlowe, Kurtz **Main Plot/Idea/Concept:** A young sailor, Marlowe, joins a Belgian trading company and goes deep into Africa to meet a man named Kurtz. Kurtz, who had established himself with natives as a kind of god, had descended into madness. **Tags:** frame story, imperialism (arrogance of imperialism), madness, wastefulness, quest
Billy Budd (Billy Budd, Sailor) by Herman Melville, published 1924	**Genre:** novel **Setting:** 1797, four years into the Napoleonic Wars; an English warship, the *Bellipotent*, somewhere on the Mediterranean Sea **Main characters:** Billy Budd and Claggert **Main Plot/Idea/Concept:** Billy's natural innocence and goodness comes in conflict with evil, in the character of Claggert. **Tags:** Christian allegory, tale of the sea, individual vs. society, good vs. evil

Continued →

(Continued from previous page)

The Scarlet Letter by Nathaniel Hawthorne, published 1850	**Genre:** novel, romantic **Setting:** mid 17th century, Boston, Massachusetts **Main characters:** Hester Prynne, Arthur Dimmesdale, Roger Chillingworth **Main Plot/Idea/Concept:** A young woman whose husband is abroad, has an affair and gives birth to a child out of wedlock. She is publicly shunned by her Puritan society and forced to wear a scarlet letter "A" that stands for adulterer. The father of the child cannot bring himself to admit his role and must deal with his oppressive guilt. **Tags:** symbolism, morality, guilt, self-sacrifice
The Great Gatsby by F. Scott Fitzgerald, published 1925	**Genre:** novel, novel of manners **Setting:** summer of 1922, New York City and Long Island, New York **Main characters:** Nick Carraway (narrator), Jay Gatsby, Daisy Buchanan **Main Plot/Idea/Concept:** Gatsby has accumulated a vast fortune so he may earn the affections of a woman of the "upper class," Daisy Buchanan, but his mysterious past stands in the way of his being accepted by her. **Tags:** 1920s, disparity among social classes, decline of the American Dream

The Awakening by Kate Chopin, published 1899	**Genre:** novel **Setting:** 1899, Grand Isle, a popular summer vacation spot for wealthy Creoles from New Orleans. The second half of the novel is set in New Orleans, primarily in the French Quarter. **Main characters:** Edna Pontellier, Robert Lebrun, Adèle **Main Plot/Idea/Concept:** On vacation, Edna experiences a series of realizations and begins a quest for independence and self-fulfillment, but social conventions that limit her self-expression prove too much for her. **Tags:** feminism, self determination, power of self-expression
Catch-22 by Joseph Heller, published 1961	**Genre:** novel **Setting:** Pianosa, a small island off the coast of Italy, near the end of World War II Main character: John Yossarian, an Air Force captain and bombardier **Main Plot/Idea/Concept:** Yossarian struggles to stay alive, despite the many parties who seem to want him dead. **Tags:** satire, loss of religious faith, power of bureaucracy, symbolism

Continued →

(Continued from previous page)

Light in August by William Faulkner, published 1932	**Genre:** novel **Setting:** 1920s in Jefferson, Mississippi and surrounding area **Main characters:** Joe Christmas, Gail Hightower, Lena Grove, Byron Bunch **Main Plot/Idea/Concept:** Joe Christmas is an adopted orphan who ends up killing his overly stern father. Years later, he is punished for his crime, but in the time intervening, he struggles for self-acceptance and to find his place in the world. **Tags:** flashback, alienation, burdens of the past, sense of self
Portrait of the Artist as a Young Man by James Joyce, published 1916	**Genre:** novel, autobiographical novel **Setting:** 1882-1903, Dublin, Ireland Main character: Stephen Dedalus **Main Plot/Idea/Concept:** Stephen struggles with whether he should be loyal to his family, the church, and to Ireland, or to pursue his dream of being an artist. **Tags:** Irish independence, the church, self determination
Ceremony by Leslie Marmon Silko, published 1977	**Genre:** novel, with poetry (Native American) **Setting:** primarily Laguna Reservation in the Southwest of the United States in the years following World War II; time is circular, events are remembered and foreshadowed **Main characters:** Tayo, whites, and Emo **Main Plot/Idea/Concept:** After recovering in a veteran's hospital, Tayo returns to his reservation. He must find a way to cure his mental wounds as well as to bring rain back to his people. **Tags:** non-linear structure, tradition, clash of cultures

Their Eyes Were Watching God by Zora Neale Hurston, published 1937	**Genre:** novel (coming of age, spiritual journey) **Setting:** Florida, 1920s or 30s **Main characters:** Janie, Pheoby, Joe Starks, Tea Cake **Main Plot/Idea/Concept:** From poor plantation beginnings, Janie's quest to be her own person teaches her about love and life's joys and sorrows. **Tags:** dialect, self determination, quest, race and racism, feminism
As I Lay Dying by William Faulkner, published 1930	**Genre:** novel **Setting:** fictional Yoknapatawpha County, Mississippi, 1920s **Main characters:** Darl Bundren (Addie's son) and Anse Bundren (Addie's husband); 15 different characters tell the story in the first person **Main Plot/Idea/Concept:** The Bundren family sets out on a somewhat heroic journey to bury their mother. A series of setbacks and obstacles mar their journey. **Tags:** black humor, satire, flashback
Candide by Voltaire, French, published 1759	**Genre:** novel, adventure, satire **Setting:** 1750s, various real and fictional locations in Europe and South America **Main characters:** Candide (whose adventures and experiences are related by a third person narrator) **Main Plot/Idea/Concept:** Candide and Pangloss's optimism is challenged by numerous disasters; Candide is expelled from his home for kissing Cunégonde; he wanders the world attempting to preserve his life and reunite with his beloved. **Tags:** Satire, irony, corrupting power of money, political oppression

Continued →

(Continued from previous page)

Othello by William Shakespeare, published 1622	**Genre:** play, tragedy **Setting:** Venice **Main characters:** Othello, Desdemona, Iago, Roderigo **Main Plot/Idea/Concept:** Despite their differences in age, race, and experience, Othello and Desdemona marry and attempt to build a life together. The envious Iago attempts to sabotage their marriage by convincing Othello that Desdemona has been unfaithful. **Tags:** seeing and blindness, revenge, race
Song of Solomon by Toni Morrison, published 1977	**Genre:** novel **Setting:** 1931-1963, Michigan, Pennsylvania, and Virginia **Main characters:** Milkman Dead, Pilate Dead, Macon Jr. **Main Plot/Idea/Concept:** Milkman Dead tries to leave the confinement of his parents' home to become independent. However, restrictions of wealth and class, as well as ignorance of his family history, become impediments. **Tags:** adventure, magical realism, allusion (Biblical), racism
Anna Karenina by Leo Tolstoy, published 1873–1877 (serial publication)	**Genre:** novel **Setting:** 1870s, primarily Russia, including Moscow, St. Petersburg, and the provinces **Main characters:** Anna Karenina; Konstantin Levin, Vronsky **Main Plot/Idea/Concept:** Anna's battle is between her passion for Vronsky and her desire for independence and her marital duty, social convention, and maternal love. **Tags:** adultery, psychological novel, tragedy, self determination

Antigone by Sophocles, written c. 441 BCE	**Genre:** drama, tragedy **Setting:** ancient Greece, Thebes **Main characters:** Antigone **Main Plot/Idea/Concept:** The major conflict is between Creon and Antigone. Creon has declared that the body of Polynices may not be given a proper burial because he led the forces that invaded Thebes. Nevertheless, Antigone wishes to give her brother a proper burial. **Tags:** individual vs society, tragedy, feminism
Bless Me, Ultima by Rudolfo Anaya, published 1972	**Genre:** novel **Setting:** New Mexico in the 1940s, during and after World War II **Main characters:** Antonio (first person narrator) **Main Plot/Idea/Concept:** This is the story of Antonio's growth from child to adolescent. Cultural traditions and his own family's expectations sometimes conflict with his own desire to be independent. **Tags:** Bildungsroman (coming-of-age story); magical realism
Death of a Salesman by Arthur Miller, published 1949	**Genre:** play **Setting:** 1940s, Brooklyn, New York, New York City, and Boston **Main characters:** Willy Loman, Linda (his wife), Biff and Happy (his two sons) **Main Plot/Idea/Concept:** A washed-up salesman considers the value of his life and decides he can leave more to his family if he's dead and his insurance check provides for them. **Tags:** tragedy, The American Dream, flashback

Continued →

(Continued from previous page)

The Glass Menagerie by Tennessee Williams, published 1945	**Genre:** play **Setting:** 1937, St. Louis **Main characters:** The Wingfield family: Tom, Laura, and their mother Amanda **Main Plot/Idea/Concept:** The family's situation is revealed through Tom's memories. Tom worries he will have to work at a meaningless job instead of writing poetry, which is more satisfying. Amanda is worried that Laura, who wears a brace on her leg and is overly shy, will never find a suitor. **Tags:** tragedy, family drama, symbolism, alienation
Jude the Obscure by Thomas Hardy, first serialized, then published as a book in 1894	**Genre:** novel **Setting:** Southwest England **Main characters:** Jude Fawley, Arabella Donn, Sue Bridehead, Mr. Phillotson **Main Plot/Idea/Concept:** Jude Fawley is a stonemason who desires to be a scholar, and toward that end, teaches himself Greek and Latin. Before he can try to enter the university, he marries an unrefined local girl, Arabella Donn, but she deserts him within two years. He moves to Christminster and meets Sue Bridehead, his cousin, who becomes the love of his life. However, she marries Mr. Phillotson. Sue is unhappy in this marriage, partly because she loves Jude, so she leaves her husband and goes to live, unmarried, with Jude. Jude and Sue have several children together and are ostracized for their behavior. **Tags:** marriage, conventional morality, individualism

The Jungle by Upton Sinclair, published 1906	**Genre:** novel (social criticism, muckraking) **Setting:** 1900, Packingtown, the meat packing section of Chicago **Main characters:** Jurgis Rudkus, Ona Lukoszaite, Teta Elzbieta Lukoszaite, Marija Berczynskas, and Phil Connor **Main Plot/Idea/Concept:** Jurgis Rudkus, a Lithuanian immigrant, and his extended family hope that by working hard they can share in the American Dream, but wage slavery and the oppression of capitalism turn their lives into tragedy. **Tags:** corruption, traditional values, symbolism, immigrant experience, evils of capitalism
Lord Jim by Joseph Conrad, published 1900	**Genre:** novel **Setting:** Indonesia **Main characters:** Jim (Lord Jim), Marlow **Main Plot/Idea/Concept:** A young British seaman named Jim becomes first mate on the *Patna*, a ship full of pilgrims traveling to Mecca. There is an accident and Jim, along with the captain and some others in the crew, abandons the ship and its passengers, a cowardly action for which he is eventually tried. It is at the trial that he meets Marlow, a sea captain who becomes Jim's friend and mentor. Marlow is the story's narrator. Jim's life toggles between his desire for redemption and his need to distance himself from the shame of his past. **Tags:** quest, human weakness, redemption

Continued →

(Continued from previous page)

Native Son by Richard Wright, published 1940	**Genre:** novel (social protest) **Setting:** 1930s, Chicago **Main characters:** Bigger Thomas, Mary Dalton, Jan Erlone, Boris Max (narrated from Bigger's perspective) **Main Plot/Idea/Concept:** A young black man gets a job as a chauffeur for the Daltons, a wealthy white family. Bigger accidentally kills Mary and he flees, but is eventually caught and put on trial. **Tags:** oppression of racism, anti-Semitism, Communism, justice,
A Passage to India by E. M. Forster, published 1924	**Genre:** political novel **Setting:** Chandrapore, India, early 20th century **Main characters:** Dr. Aziz, Mrs. Moore, Miss Adela Quested, Ronny Heaslop **Main Plot/Idea/Concept:** Miss Quested accuses Dr. Aziz of attempting to sexually assault her in the nearby Marabar Caves. Aziz suspects Fielding of plotting against him with the English. **Tags:** colonialism
Beloved by Toni Morrison, published 1987	**Genre:** novel (historical fiction) **Setting:** 1873, with flashbacks to the early 1850s, Cincinnati, Ohio, Kentucky, and Alfred, Georgia **Main characters:** Sethe, Denver, and Paul D., Beloved, Baby Suggs **Main Plot/Idea/Concept:** Sethe escapes from slavery, but kills her older daughter to keep her from being taken back to the South by her old master. A mysterious figure appears at Sethe's home, calling herself by the name on the dead daughter's tombstone. **Tags:** supernatural, oppressive effects of slavery

The *Color Purple* by Alice Walker, published 1982	**Genre:** novel (epistolary) **Setting:** rural Georgia, 1910-1940 **Main characters:** Celie, Shug, Nettie **Main Plot/Idea/Concept:** Celie is verbally, physically, and sexually abused by several different men, lowering her self esteem; she is a child woman with no voice, and no one to turn to. The story is told through a series of letters in Celie's voice. **Tags:** racism, sexism, self discovery
The Crucible by Arthur Miller	**Genre:** play **Setting:** Salem, Massachusetts **Main characters:** John and Elizabeth Proctor, Thomas and Ann Putnam, Reverend Parris, Abigail Williams, and Reverend John Hale **Main Plot/Idea/Concept:** Abigail Williams leads a group of young girls who accuse local men and women of witchcraft partly to cover up their "sinful" nocturnal activities in the forest. John Proctor, who has committed adultery with Abigail Williams, tries to combat the hysteria. **Tags:** intolerance, greed, sin and forgiveness, tragedy, McCarthy Hearings (Red Scare) Note: Miller's play is based on real characters in the Salem Witch Trials

Continued →

(Continued from previous page)

Cry, The Beloved Country by Alan Paton, published 1948	**Genre:** novel **Setting:** 1940s, Ndotsheni and Johannesburg, South Africa **Main characters:** Stephen Kumalo, James Jarvis, Theophilus Msimangu, Absalom Kumalo, Arthur Jarvis **Main Plot/Idea/Concept:** Stephen Kumalo struggles against white oppression and the corrupting influences of city life that are destroying his family and his country. He travels to Johannesburg to search for his son who has been arrested for the murder of Arthur Jarvis. However, he is unable to save his son, who is sentenced to death. Afterward, Jarvis' father helps Kumalo to improve conditions in the village. **Tags:** Apartheid, fathers and sons, injustice, repentance
A Doll's House by Henrik Ibsen, first published 1879	**Genre:** play **Setting:** Norway, late 1800s **Main characters:** Nora and Torvald Helmer, Kristine Lind, Dr. Rank, Nils Krogstad **Main Plot/Idea/Concept:** A young wife, who has forged her father's signature to gain funds to take her ill husband on a rest cure, finds herself about to be found out, a result that would bring shame upon her husband and threaten her marriage. **Tags:** women's rights, honor/duty, gender roles, marriage

An Enemy of the People by Henrik Ibsen, published 1882	**Genre:** play **Setting:** 19th century coastal Norway **Main characters:** Dr. Thomas Stockmann, Peter Stockmann **Main Plot/Idea/Concept:** The town the Stockmanns live in has just invested a lot of money in new public baths, which they hope will pay off through an increase in tourism. The baths become popular and lucrative, but Dr. Stockmann discovers that waste from the local tannery is polluting the baths and making them toxic to users. Far from being rewarded for his community-minded act, Stockmann is ostracized for his unwillingness to go along with the cover-up. **Tags:** hypocrisy of political systems; disillusionment; illusion of truth
Ethan Frome by Edith Wharton, published 1911	**Genre:** novel **Setting:** Massachusetts, late 19th and early 20th centuries **Main characters:** Ethan Frome, Zenobia (Zeena) Frome, Mattie Silver **Main Plot/Idea/Concept:** Ethan Frome is a married man who cannot act upon his feelings for another woman. **Tags:** social oppression, marriage
Hedda Gabler by Henrik Ibsen, published 1890	**Genre:** play **Setting:** Norway, 19th century **Main characters:** Hedda Gabler, Jørgen Tesman, Miss Juliane Tesman, Mrs. Thea Elvsted **Main Plot/Idea/Concept:** Newly married Hedda does not love her husband and her new life with him bores her. Her husband's old rival reappears and threatens their economic security. **Tags:** feminism, self determination, jealousy, suicide, dissatisfaction with marriage

Continued →

(Continued from previous page)

Obasan by Joy Kogawa, published 1981	**Genre:** novel (historical) **Setting:** 1972 and World War II, Canada **Main characters:** Naomi Nakane, Obasan, Aunt Emily, Stephen **Main Plot/Idea/Concept:** Naomi struggles to reconcile herself with her painful past. **Tags:** Japanese Canadian relocation, World War II, clash of cultures
Portrait of a Lady by Henry James, serialized 1880-81, published as a book in 1881	**Genre:** novel **Setting:** Europe (England and Italy, primarily) **Main characters:** Isabel Archer, Gilbert Osmond, Pansy Main Plot/Idea/Concept Isabel Archer inherits a fortune, but must fight to control her own destiny. **Tags:** old vs. new world, personal freedom, betrayal
A Raisin in the Sun by Lorraine Hansberry, published 1950	**Genre:** play **Setting:** Chicago **Main characters:** Walter and Beneatha Younger, their mother, and Walter's wife, Ruth **Main Plot/Idea/Concept:** A family has different views on how to spend an insurance settlement. They also fight against racial prejudice. **Tags:** dignity and honor, racism, gender roles, cultural assimilation
Rosencrantz and Guildenstern Are Dead by Tom Stoppard, published 1967	**Genre:** play **Setting:** late 1500s, Hamlet's court **Main characters:** Rosencrantz and Guildenstern **Main Plot/Idea/Concept:** Rosencrantz and Guildenstern try to discover the cause of Hamlet's madness and, at the same time, their own purpose in the world. **Tags:** satire, black comedy, making choices

The Sound and the Fury by William Faulkner, published 1929	**Genre:** novel **Setting:** Easter weekend, 1928, and June 1929 (with flashbacks); Jefferson, Mississippi, and Cambridge, Massachusetts (Harvard University) **Main characters:** children of the Compson family: Benjy, Quentin, Jason, and Caddie, Quentin (Caddie's daughter), and housekeeper Dilsey **Main Plot/Idea/Concept:** A distinguished family falls from grace. **Tags:** nihilism, order and chaos, time, structure (four different narrators), stream of consciousness
A Streetcar Named Desire by Tennessee Williams, published 1947	**Genre:** play **Setting:** 1940s, New Orleans, Louisiana **Main characters:** Blanche DuBois, Stanley Kowalski **Main Plot/Idea/Concept:** Blanche DuBois, an aging Southern debutante, tries to flee a sordid past when she comes to live with her sister in New Orleans. She hopes to begin again and reclaim her "glory," but she is pitted against working class Stanley Kowalski, her sister's husband. **Tags:** tragedy
The Sun Also Rises by Ernest Hemingway, published 1926	**Genre:** novel **Setting:** Paris, France, and Pamplona and Madrid, Spain: 1924 **Main characters:** Jake Barnes, Brett Ashley **Main Plot/Idea/Concept:** Jake loves Lady Brett Ashley, but his impotence caused by a war wound hinders their relationship. Jake loses numerous friendships, and his life is repeatedly disrupted, because of his loyalty to Brett, who has a destructive series of love affairs with other men. **Tags:** Lost Generation, disillusionment

Continued →

(Continued from previous page)

The Tempest by William Shakespeare	**Genre:** play **Setting:** the Renaissance, on an island probably off the coast of Italy **Main characters:** Prospero, Miranda, Ariel, Calaban **Main Plot/Idea/Concept:** Prospero, the duke of Milan and a powerful magician, is banished from Italy and cast out to sea by his brother, Antonio, and Alonso, the king of Naples. Prospero seeks to use his magic to make these lords repent and restore him to his rightful place. **Tags:** the theater, magic, revenge
Waiting for Godot by Samuel Beckett, first produced in 1953	**Genre:** two-act play **Setting:** a country road by a tree, 20th century **Main characters:** Estragon, Vladimir, Pozzo and Lucky **Main Plot/Idea/Concept:** Two men wait unsuccessfully for someone named Godot to arrive. They say he is an acquaintance but, in fact, hardly know him, admitting that they would not recognize him if they saw him. To occupy themselves, they eat, sleep, talk, argue, play games, and contemplate suicide—anything "to hold the terrible silence at bay." **Tags:** existentialism, life is a game

All the King's Men by Robert Penn Warren, published 1946 (won Pulitzer Prize in 1947)	**Genre:** novel **Setting:** 1930s, the American South **Main characters:** Willie Stark, Jack Burden, Anne Stanton, Adam Stanton **Main Plot/Idea/Concept:** Willie Stark turns from an idealistic lawyer into a charismatic and powerful governor. On his way, Stark embraces various forms of corruption and builds an enormous political machine based on patronage and intimidation. His approach to politics earns him many enemies in the state legislature, but his constituents are nonetheless drawn to his fervent populist manner. **Tags:** Huey Long, political corruption, nihilism, Calvinism, charismatic public figures
All the Pretty Horses by Cormac McCarthy, published 1992 (first book of *The Border Trilogy;* received National Book Award)	**Genre:** novel **Setting:** Texas, Mexico, 1949 **Main characters:** John Grady Cole, Lacey Rawlins, Jimmy Blevins, and Alejandra **Main Plot/Idea/Concept:** Sixteen-year-old John Grady Cole grew up on his grandfathers' ranch. After his grandfather's death, Cole learns the ranch is to be sold. He cannot face the idea of living in town, so he convinces his best friend to travel to Mexico, hoping they will find work as cowboys. **Tags:** coming of age, loss of innocence, the nature of evil

Continued →

(Continued from previous page)

Frankenstein by Mary Shelley, published 1818	**Genre:** novel **Setting:** 18th century Europe **Main characters:** Narrator: Robert Walton (in letters to his sister), Victor Frankenstein **Main Plot/Idea/Concept:** In college, Victor Frankenstein excels at the sciences and discovers the secret to giving life to the inanimate. He eventually creates his "monster." This classic novel explores the results of unchecked ambition. **Tags:** science fiction, horror, effects of ambition
Gulliver's Travels by Jonathan Swift, published 1726	**Genre:** satire (fictional narrative) **Setting:** early 18th century, primarily in Great Britain, but also in fictional lands such as Brobdingnag **Main characters:** Lemuel Gulliver, narrator **Main Plot/Idea/Concept:** Gulliver, a British surgeon, turns sea captain in four voyages that reveal to him the worst of human nature. **Tags:** satire, fantasy, adventure, politics
Hamlet by William Shakespeare, written between 1599 and 1601	**Genre:** play **Setting:** medieval Denmark **Main characters:** Hamlet, Claudius, Polonius, Ophelia **Main Plot/Idea/Concept:** The ghost of the murdered king of Denmark asks his son Hamlet to avenge his death. **Tags:** foreshadowing, death and suicide, uncertainty of the future, treachery, moral corruption

Madame Bovary by Gustave Flaubert, serialized October 1, 1856, and December 15, 1856, tried for obscenity which made it notorious, published as a novel in 1857	**Genre:** novel **Setting:** 19th century provincial France **Main characters:** Emma Bovary, Charles Bovary, Monsier and Madame Homais, Léon Dupuis, and Rodolphe Boulanger **Main Plot/Idea/Concept:** Emma Bovary is discontented with marriage, which leads her into a scandalous affair. Her spend-thrift ways leave her husband in financial distress, but she finds she relies on his generosity and tries to help him. **Tags:** realism, Flaubert's greatest work
The Mayor of Casterbridge by Thomas Hardy, serialized first, then published 1886	**Genre:** novel **Setting:** fictional Casterbridge, mid 1800s **Main characters:** Michael Henchard, Donald Farfrae, Susan Henchard, Elizabeth-Jane Newson **Main Plot/Idea/Concept:** One night, drunk and angry with his wife, Henchard sells his wife and child to a sailor. After the sailor dies, Susan returns with her daughter and reunites with her former husband. **Tags:** honor, moral righteousness, reconciliation
Medea by Euripides, 431 BCE	**Genre:** play, Greek tragedy **Setting:** Corinth **Main characters:** Medea, Jason, King Creon (of Corinth), and Glauce, Creon's daughter **Main Plot/Idea/Concept:** Medea's husband Jason has turned her and her children away so he can marry King Creon's daughter, in hopes of advancing his social station. **Tags:** revenge, murder, tragedy

Continued →

(Continued from previous page)

The Merchant of Venice by William Shakespeare, from 1596-98	**Genre:** play, comedy **Setting:** Venice **Main characters:** Antonio (a merchant), Shylock (a moneylender and a Jew), Bassanio, Lorenzo, Portia, Jessica and Nerissa **Main Plot/Idea/Concept:** Bassanio wishes to court the wealthy Portia, but he's squandered his fortune. He asks his friend Antonio to help him once again, but Antonio's fortune is tied up in his ships out to sea, so they engage the money lender, Shylock. The condition of the loan, if it is not repaid, is that Shylock may take a pound of flesh from Antonio. **Tags:** anti-Semitism, disguise, gender roles, marriage, Portia's famous speech on mercy
Moll Flanders by Daniel Defoe, 1722	**Genre:** novel, episodic **Setting:** London, Virginia **Main characters:** Moll, her mother, numerous men, some of whom she marries **Main Plot/Idea/Concept:** The full title says it all: "The Fortunes and Misfortunes of the Famous Moll Flanders, Etc. Who was born in Newgate, and during a life of continu'd Variety for Threescore Years, besides her Childhood, was Twelve Year a Whore, five times a Wife (whereof once to her own brother), Twelve Year a Thief, Eight Year a Transported Felon in Virginia, at last grew Rich, liv'd Honest and died a Penitent. Written from her own Memorandums." **Tags:** alienation of lower classes, poverty, adventure, marriage, self-determination

Mrs. Dalloway by Virginia Woolf, published 1925	**Genre:** novel **Setting:** England, post World War I **Main characters:** Clarissa Dalloway, Septimus Smith **Main Plot/Idea/Concept:** All of the present action takes place on one day in June. The author uses flashbacks to other times and locales. Mrs. Dalloway prepares for a party and thinks of her marriage and those she has loved. **Tags:** stream of consciousness, feminism, homosexuality, value of inner life (thoughts, emotions), effects of war
Murder in the Cathedral by T. S. Eliot, first performed in 1935	**Genre:** poetic drama **Setting:** Canterbury, England, 1170 (when Archbishop Thomas Becket was murdered) in the archbishop's hall and in the cathedral **Main characters:** Chorus, as in a Greek drama, comments on the action in the play. The archbishop, himself, knights, three tempters. **Main Plot/Idea/Concept:** Thomas Becket is murdered and martyred. **Tags:** individual versus authority, anti-fascism, power of church versus state
Pride and Prejudice by Jane Austen, published 1813	**Genre:** novel **Setting:** Hertfordshire, England, turn of the century **Main characters:** Elizabeth Bennet, second eldest of a poor country gentleman, Mr. Darcy, George Wickam, and Jane Bennet **Main Plot/Idea/Concept:** The novel chronicles the experiences of the Bennet sisters and their love interests. **Tags:** social class, morality and moral judgment, manners, and marriage

Continued →

(Continued from previous page)

Sula by Toni Morrison, published 1973	**Genre:** novel **Setting:** The Bottom, a predominantly black community in Ohio, from 1919-1965 **Main characters:** Shadrack, Eva Peace, Hannah Peace, Sula Peace, Nel Wright and Tar Baby **Main Plot/Idea/Concept:** Agriculturally worthless land given to blacks eventually becomes valuable to whites, who want to turn it into a golf course. However, the setting serves primarily as an anchor for the story of the Peace family and their friends and neighbors over the years. **Tags:** racism, poverty and hopelessness, good and evil, post war stress
Tess of the D'Urbervilles by Thomas Hardy, published 1891	**Genre:** novel (Victorian) **Setting:** late 19th century **Main characters:** Tess Durbeyfield, Alec D'Urberville, Angel Clare **Main Plot/Idea/Concept:** Thinking they are "lost" aristocracy, the poor Derbyfields send Tess to state their case to the wealthy D'Urbervilles. There she is seduced by the unscrupulous Alec and becomes pregnant. After the baby dies, Tess tries to find her own way, eventually meeting and falling in love with Angel, but her past does not allow her to be happy. **Tags:** injustice, powerlessness, symbolism

The Turn of the Screw by Henry James, published 1898	**Genre:** short novel, novella **Setting:** 1840s, Bly, a country home in Essex, England **Main characters:** Douglas, Flora, the governess, Mrs. Grose, Miss Jessel, Miles, Peter Quint **Main Plot/Idea/Concept:** The story is narrated by the governess who fears the children in her care are being tormented by ghosts. **Tags:** psychological novel, ghost story, sexual repression, madness
Who's Afraid of Virginia Woolf? by Edward Albee, first performed in 1962	**Genre:** play **Setting:** small New England university **Main characters:** George, Martha, Honey, and Nick **Main Plot/Idea/Concept:** George and Martha invite new professor Nick and his wife to their home after a party, where everyone had been drinking. George and Martha verbally abuse each other in front of their guests. In this play the illusion of 1950s perfection is exploded. **Tags:** marriage, social norms
Wide Sargasso Sea by Jean Rhys, published 1964–66	**Genre:** novel **Setting:** 1840s, Jamaica, the Windward Islands, England **Main characters:** Antoinette, Mr. Rochester, Christophine **Main Plot/Idea/Concept:** Rhys creates the unknown story of Bertha Mason, the insane wife of Edward Rochester in Charlotte Brontë's novel *Jane Eyre*. Mason, born Antoinette Cosway, is the daughter of former slave owners in Jamaica. **Tags:** colonialism and clashes of culture, slavery, race, religion, symbolism, written as prequel to Jane Eyre

REMEMBERING MAJOR WORKS

Use this sheet to review a major work you have read that you might use for question three on the AP Lit exam.

Title:

Author:

Genre:

Literary Period, if significant:

Historical significance:

Setting: (time, place, and atmosphere, especially if the setting is a major element in the work)

Protagonist: (name, personality, appearance, etc.)

Antagonist(s):

Main conflict: (think in terms of what the protagonist wants/desires and what is keeping him/her from getting it).

Brief plot summary:

Resolution (of main conflict):

Major Themes: (What truths about life/human nature are revealed?)

Symbols:

Remarkable events/images/other elements:

Chapter

5

Six Elements of Style:
Diction, Imagery, Tone, Syntax, Point of View, and Figurative Language

In This Chapter

Overview

Diction
Connotation
Denotation
Style
Some typical style descriptors

Imagery
Types of imagery
Effects of imagery

Tone
Mood

Syntax
Sentence types and attributes
More aspects of syntax
The 3P's of syntax

Point of View
Main points of view

Figurative Language
How to recognize figurative language
Specific types of figurative language

Style descriptors
More style and tone words

OVERVIEW

Every AP Lit exam will have questions about six main elements of style. It is important to know them for the multiple-choice section as well as for the essays. If you could study nothing else in preparation for the AP Lit exam, this would be the chapter to study.

It is far better, of course, to be familiar with all the concepts in this book as they work interdependently. So, as you read and study the other chapters, return to this one often to reinforce the big six!

DICTION

Diction is often defined as the *author's choice of words*.

There are two ways to think of diction:

1) Specific effect of word choice: connotation and denotation

2) Overall style

CONNOTATION

In analyzing word choice, you are looking at the connotation of a specific word choice and the effect of that association on the passage. Connotation is the *emotional* sense of a word or the *cultural meaning* associated with a word. Connotations evoke associations. For example, the word "cancer" evokes fear, trepidation, and more.

In the passage from Cormac McCarthy's *The Crossing* (featured on the AP Lit exam, 1999), the author evokes a reverent tone, partly through his word choice. Words like "scrim," "celebrants," "sacred," "sects," and "penitent" have religious connotations. Careful readers will make spiritual associations, which will help them connect with one of the main themes of the passage, which is that all living creatures, whether animal or human, are eternally connected through spirit.

Test Tip

Connotation: A Simple Strategy: When you read, if you begin to notice several words that fit together in connotative meaning, make a list of them in the margin (or circle them in the text). You are noticing a series of words that create a dominant impression. While this impression may not drive an essay thesis, it is probably a key to understanding that is worth noting.

DENOTATION

Denotation refers to the *dictionary or precise meaning* of a word. Authors' use of the right word for the passage can be key to their clarity of expression. Knowing a wide variety of words and their meanings is critical to understanding complex prose passages or even poetry.

One of the main reasons students misread a poem or a passage is that they do not understand the vocabulary in the text. Unfortunately, you won't be able to consult a dictionary when you are taking the exam. Please see a list of potentially difficult vocabulary words in Chapter 9.

It is also important to be open-minded regarding the meanings of words. Be careful to not automatically attribute a common meaning to a word, especially when you are reading older texts, as meanings of words change over time. For example, the word "terrific" means "wonderful or great" in a contemporary context, but in the context in which it appears on a released exam, it means "terrifying." Another example is the word "awful," which means in its context "to be in awe of," but a careless reader might think it simply means "horrible."

To avoid misreading a text, especially when confronted with archaic language, try to determine word meanings from the broader context of the text.

Test Tip *Archaic, obscure, or overly specific language in poems or prose passages will generally be defined in footnotes.*

STYLE

Word choice also impacts overall style. Think of style as the *voice of the writer*. Many decisions a writer makes—such as types and lengths of sentences (see syntax), types of words used (see diction), and the extent to which he or she uses imagery and figurative language—contribute to what is recognized as his or her style. For example, Hemingway's style is characterized, in part, by short, simple sentence structure, while William Faulkner is known for excessively long sentences.

Style can also mean something similar to tone.

Consider the difference in the styles of these two examples:

    A) She was like, pizza is so, like, fattening. (Casual, conversational)

    B) She understood that pizza was excessively high in fat and calories. (Formal)

You will be expected to understand that style impacts other elements in a passage, like characterization, attitude of speaker, and more. In the examples above, the speaker of example A could be said to be less intelligent than the speaker of example B.

SOME TYPICAL STYLE DESCRIPTORS:

Authoritative: the voice is commanding and knowing

Emotive: the voice evokes emotion

Didactic: the voice is preachy, insistent

Objective: the voice is uncommitted, without judgment

Ornate: the voice is perhaps pretentious, flowery, or ostentatious

Plain: the voice is simple, straightforward, to the point

Scholarly: the voice is learned and authoritative, erudite

Scientific: the voice is precise and relies on the language of science (Latinate words)

You'll find a more comprehensive list of style descriptors at the end of this chapter.

IMAGERY

Imagery is not just one of the most important elements of poetry, it is also important to prose writers. Imagery is *language that engages the senses and evokes emotion*. We relate to imagery on a gut level, responding with our emotions. The more detailed the imagery, the more we can put ourselves into the writing.

TYPES OF IMAGERY

- Visual Imagery: what we can see

- Auditory: what we can hear

- Tactile: what we can touch

- Olfactory: what we can smell

- Gustatory: what we can taste

- Kinesthetic: sense of movement

- Organic: internal sense of being (well or ill)

These sensory perceptions created through language are vicarious (through the experience of the character or the narration). We might also consider these perceptions to be virtual. We don't actually experience them, but the emotions they evoke in us are real—the more vivid the imagery, the more real the emotion.

To become good at recognizing good imagery, become good at looking for it and studying it. Stop when you recognize a particularly imagistic passage. Study it. What kind of imagery is it? How do you feel as you experience the passage? And most important, what is the effect of the imagery?

EFFECTS OF IMAGERY

- Helps establish tone

- Creates realistic settings

- Creates empathy in readers for characters

- Helps readers imagine themselves as part of a narrative

TONE

Tone is *the attitude of the speaker toward another character, a place, an idea or a thing.* In thinking of tone in this regard, it is important to pay attention not only to what a character or speaker does, but also to what he or she says. Sometimes we know more than the character does (dramatic irony) and this impacts our understanding of tone.

A passage or paragraph has a specific tone, which refers to its emotional quality. This quality comes from details like imagery, diction (a character's speech, for example), and even syntax (short, simple sentences seem more serious and less reflective than more ornate sentence types).

Tone is created in a variety of ways. Diction and imagery are major influences on tone. This is because images evoke emotions and certain words have emotional connotations. When you recognize tone, you most likely "feel" it first. But you also have to have an intellectual understanding of what you feel.

The first key to analyzing tone is to recognize it. You must acquaint yourself with typical tone descriptors (see the list at the end of this chapter), so that you aren't fumbling for a word to express what you think you see. The wider the variety of tone descriptors you use, the better you'll be at providing a precise analysis. In other words, if you say a passage is *sad* instead of *melancholy,* you may be limiting your analysis.

MOOD

Mood is related to tone. The term "mood" is most often used in association with setting. Think of mood as *the emotional quality of the setting.*

While there is most likely a prominent or dominant tone in a passage, be aware of tone shifts. If the tone changes suddenly, it can signal an epiphany or some change in a speaker or character's thinking. Tone shifts are critical markers in a passage.

See the end of this chapter for a comprehensive list of words to use when describing tone and mood.

SYNTAX

Syntax refers, in general, to *the order of words in a sentence.* Syntax results in various sentence types used for a variety of rhetorical effects. Syntax can also be thought of as the rhythm of prose. Sentence variety creates interesting, fluent, readable prose. Aspects of syntax, such as repetition and placement of ideas, are used for emphasis.

A study of syntax is important for several reasons.

- Sentences impact the narrative pace of a passage, making it read quickly or slowly, which therefore impacts the idea/ theme

- Certain types of sentences are better at emphasizing ideas, so key notions become prominent through repetition or parallel structure

- There are sometimes questions in the multiple-choice section of the exam that ask you to identify types of sentences

SENTENCE TYPES AND ATTRIBUTES

Sentence type	Attributes
Periodic	The most important idea comes at the end of the sentence.
Loose	The most important idea is revealed early and the sentence unfolds loosely after that.
Parallel	A parallel sentence (sometimes called a balanced sentence) contains parts of equal grammatical structure or rhetorical value in a variety of combinations. Some examples of parallel structures: 1. The dog ate voraciously, joyously, and noisily. (The verb *ate* is modified by three multisyllabic adverbs, which seems somewhat lofty in style for such a mundane act as a dog eating.) 2. Joyce was worn down by the constant invasion of her co-workers, by their insistent stares, by their noisy whispers, and by their unveiled disdain. She knew she had to find another job. (The parallel phrases are set off by commas; this is also an example of anaphora.)

Continued ➔

(Continued from previous page)

Sentence type	Attributes
Repetition	Types of repetition in sentences: **Anaphora:** the repetition of the same word or words at the beginning of a series of phrases, clauses, or sentences **Antistrophe:** the repetition of the same word or words at the end of successive phrases or clauses **Asyndeton:** conjunctions are omitted between words, phrases, or clauses **Chiasmus:** two corresponding pairs ordered this way a/b/b/a **Polysyndeton:** the use of conjunctions between each word, phrase, or clause
Grammatical sentence types	1. Simple: 1 subject, 1 verb, modifiers, complements. Simple sentences are short, direct, and in combination with more complex sentences can be used for emphasis. 2. Compound: 2 independent clauses joined by a coordinating conjunction (use the mnemonic "fanboys:" _f_or, _a_nd, _n_or, _b_ut, _o_r, _y_et, _s_o) 3. Complex: contains an independent clause and a (dependent) subordinate clause 4. Compound-complex: contains two independent clauses and a dependent (subordinate) clause
Grammatical sentence purposes	1. Declarative sentence: makes a statement. 2. Imperative sentence: makes a command. 3. Interrogative sentence: asks a question. 4. Exclamatory sentence: makes an emphatic or emotion-filled statement.

MORE ASPECTS OF SYNTAX

1. Climax: the main idea or most important point in a sentence. The position of the climax may be varied for effect.

2. Cadence: the rhythm or "music" of a sentence that comes through parallel elements and repetition

3. Narrative pace: the pace or speed of a passage that comes through the following elements:

   - length of words

   - omission of words or punctuation

   - length of sentences

   - number of dependent/subordinate clauses

   - repetition of sounds

The shorter the words (fewer syllables) and the shorter and simpler the sentences, the faster the pace. Conversely, the longer the words (more syllables) and the longer, more complex the sentences, the slower the pace.

The 3 P's of Syntax

Prominence: Prominence refers to *the importance given an idea in a sentence*. Prominence is achieved both by placement and by repetition. Sometimes an idea is isolated in a short sentence where it is given sole prominence. If a word is ever set off alone as a fragment, it is being given prominence that best not be ignored. Instead, ask the question, "Why is this word isolated?"

Position: Position means *where the key idea is located*. It will most often come at the beginning of the sentence (loose sentence) or at the end of the sentence (periodic sentence). But sometimes, writers use nonstandard syntax, or inverted word order (especially in poems), to draw attention to certain words or ideas.

Continued →

(Continued from previous page)

Pace: Pace is *the speed of the text* and generally complements the author's purpose. For example: Quentin's section in Faulkner's *The Sound and The Fury* is presented primarily in stream of consciousness, with fast-paced narration that emphasizes the character's frenetic and fragile state of mind. Another great example of how pace complements the writer's purpose is Maya Angelou's poem *Woman Work*. The first stanza in which she describes all the tasks to be done is meant to be read so fast that the reader actually feels tired after reading it. The rest of the poem is composed of four-line stanzas that read much, much more slowly. The images in these stanzas evoke peace, coolness, and rest.

Test Tip

Your own syntax is important in the essay section of the exam. See Chapter 15 for more on using sentence variety in your own writing.

POINT OF VIEW

Point of view is one of the most important elements of literature that you need to understand for the AP Lit exam. Most of the essay prompts imply an analysis of point of view, such as the speaker's response to an event, the speaker's attitude about an idea, etc. See Chapter 14 for a detailed analysis of prompts. Further, see Chapter 13 for more on point of view.

MAIN POINTS OF VIEW

First person: the narrator tells his/her own story using first person pronouns (*I, me, we, us*). This point of view is limited by what the narrator can know, see, or understand. First person narrators cannot always be trusted to assess the situation honestly. They may be blind to their own faults.

Second person: the narrator uses second person pronouns (*you*) to make immediate connections with readers (very rare point of view in fiction)

Third person-limited: a third person narrator tells the story from one character's point of view using third person pronouns (*she, her, he, him, it, they, them*); limited by the same constraints as first person narrators

Third person-omniscient: this third person narrator is god-like, seeing and knowing all without constraints of time or space, seeing even beyond earthly existence. Third person narrators often digress into contemplative or philosophical forays.

Objective: an objective narrator tells a story like a camcorder would, simply revealing the sights and sounds it perceives (though not, of course, as strictly as that). You can recognize an objective narrator by that person's lack of emotion or personal interest in the subject.

FIGURATIVE LANGUAGE

The last element of style is figurative language, or *language not meant to be taken literally*. If we were to narrow down figurative language to one element, it would be metaphor. But, of course, it is more than that. Being able to recognize figurative language and its effects is a key skill necessary for success on the AP Lit exam.

Authors and poets use figurative language to lead us to a deeper level of understanding and to see things in a new or even startling way. When confronted with complex metaphors, it is important to ask "what" and "why." What are we to see that we would not have seen without it? Why is it there in the first place?

HOW TO RECOGNIZE FIGURATIVE LANGUAGE

- Learn the patterns of types of figurative language so that when you encounter them, you recognize them.

- Be open to finding it: know that when a passage seems to be saying more than what appears on the surface, there is probably figurative language at work. Learn to read under the surface or, as is often said, "between the lines."

- Remember that poetry is almost a synonym for figurative language, meaning that there is a great deal of it in poetry. Always be looking for it.

- Read carefully and don't settle for the most obvious interpretation.

SPECIFIC TYPES OF FIGURATIVE LANGUAGE
(See also Chapters 6 and 7.)

Allegory: a type of symbolism. An allegory is *a description or a narrative (poetry or prose) with a secondary, or underlying, meaning*. An excellent example of allegory is George Orwell's *Animal Farm*. In that book, the situation, the characters, and the plot all have allegorical connections. (Briefly, the overthrow of a cruel farmer by the farm's animals is meant to parallel the Russian Revolution where the proletariat revolted against their dictator.)

Character allegory: In Dante's *Inferno*, characters often represent various ideal qualities. Vergil, for example, stands for human reason. This meaning extends throughout the epic.

- Human virtues and vices were common character allegories in medieval literature, though they were generalized and not necessarily specific characters.

Apostrophe (related to personification): *addressing something (or someone) non-living or incapable of response as if it could hear and respond*, such as "O, howling wind. . . ."

Irony: Irony exists when there is *a discrepancy between what is perceived and what is real.* There are three types of irony:

> **Verbal irony**—when what is said is different from what is meant
>
> **Dramatic irony**—when the reader knows something a character does not know
>
> **Situational irony**—when some aspect of the situation seems incongruous to either what seems appropriate or to what is expected

Test Tip

Being able to recognize irony and its effect is an excellent skill to cultivate. There are always several questions on the AP Lit exam regarding irony.

Metaphor: a *comparison of two dissimilar things in order to see one in a new way*

Metonymy (see also synecdoche): the *use of a closely related detail for the thing actually meant,* such as using The White House to refer to the president.

Overstatement (hyperbole): *saying more than the situation warrants.* The contrast illuminates the truth.

Paradox: a statement that consists of *two contradictory or incompatible elements*; paradoxical statements are startling and get us to think. They are a kind of metaphor that reveals the truth.

Personification: *attributing human qualities or characteristics to non-living or non-human things in order to create empathy*

Simile: essentially *a metaphor that uses "like" or "as"*

> **Epic or Homeric simile:** *an extended simile used in epic poems and Greek dramas.* A typical construction of an epic simile uses "just as" or "so then" to signal the comparison, though that is not *always* the case. The following example is from Homer's Odyssey (Fitzgerald translation):
>
> > *A man in a distant field, no hearthfires near,*
> > *will hide a fresh brand in his bed of embers*
> > *to keep a spark alive for the next day;*
> > *so in the leaves Odysseus hid himself,*
> > *while over him Athena showered sleep*
> > *that his distress should end, and soon, soon*
> > *in quiet sleep she sealed his cherished eyes.*

Synecdoche: *the use of a part for the whole,* such as "all hands on deck" or "the meeting can begin now that all the suits are here." Note: Synecdoche is sometimes represented as metonymy.

Symbol: *a thing, person, or idea that stands for something else.* Some symbols become iconic, that is, so well known that they're an accepted part of culture. Ex: water is a symbol of purity and or rebirth.

Understatement: *saying less than the situation warrants.* The contrast illuminates the truth.

Test Tip

Create an annotation symbol for metaphors, such as a star. Mark all metaphors as you read so they are easy to find and assess later.

STYLE DESCRIPTORS

The descriptors in the following lists come from questions about tone, style, attitude, and mood from released exams.

Tone

candid	laconic	sanctimonious	speculative
cynical	melancholy	sardonic	trite
detached	nostalgic	sinister	

Style

candid	detached	scornful	smug
cynical	sardonic	sinister	

Attitude

arrogant	eloquent	indifferent	vindictive
ambivalent	disdainful	pretentious	whimsical
anxious	fanciful	remorseful	
contemptuous	flippant	satirical	

Mood

apprehensive	quizzical	reproachful	solemn
elegiac	rapturous	satiric	suspenseful

MORE STYLE AND TONE WORDS

Style

accusatory	despairing	obsequious
acerbic	disdainful	patronizing
ambivalent	earnest	pessimistic
apathetic	gloomy	petulant
bitter	haughty	quizzical
conciliatory	indignant	reverent
condescending	judgmental	ridiculing
callous	jovial	reflective
contemplative	mocking	sarcastic
critical	morose, focusing on death	sardonic
choleric		self-deprecating
churlish	malicious	sincere
contemptuous	objective	solemn
derisive	optimistic	

Tone

caustic	matter-of-fact	ribald
colloquial	informal	satiric
didactic	intimate	scholarly
effusive	lyrical	terse
erudite	objective	scholarly
fanciful	pedantic	terse
formal	poignant	whimsical
forthright		

Basic Elements
of Fiction and Drama

On the AP Lit exam it won't be enough for you to simply identify literary elements. You will need to show how the elements contribute to the meaning of the work.

OVERVIEW

If doctors did not use precise medical terminology—"scalpel, stat" instead of "could you hand me that blade thing-y when you've got a moment?"—you would not want to be in surgery. It is important that doctors and nurses understand the language of their profession to do their jobs well. It is likewise important for you to understand the language we use to talk and write about literature.

The purpose of this chapter, and those that follow for poetry and language, is to define for you a **basic list** of literary terms, specifically, the literary terms that have appeared on AP Lit released exams. However, it is not enough for you just to know these terms and be able to define them. Your expert use of these terms in arguing your point about a passage is the next step. Chapter 11 will help you understand more about literary analysis. But let's start at the beginning.

KEY TERMS

It is critical to know these terms well. The starred terms (★) are those that have appeared more prominently on released AP Lit exams.

1. ★ **allusion**: a reference to something in previous literature, history, or culture that adds to or emphasizes a theme of the work

2. **allegory**: a narrative or description with a secondary or symbolic meaning underlying the literal meaning. An example of an allegory is Orwell's *Animal Farm*. Old Major, the leader of the animals' revolution, is often seen to represent Karl Marx, who urged the proletariat to revolt.

3. **anecdote**: a clever little story; a short account of an interesting situation

4. **anti hero**: a protagonist whose attributes are opposite of what is expected of heroes. Antiheroes may be confused, powerless, victimized, or simply pathetic.

5. **archetype**: a symbol that recurs often enough in literature over time to be easily recognizable, such as water as a purifying element or the sun as knowledge; also character types that are common: prodigal son, wise grandfather, etc.

6. ★ **atmosphere**: the emotional quality of the setting

7. **epiphany**: a moment of insight, spiritual or personal; a character's sudden revelation about life or his or her own circumstances

8. **eulogy**: a speech given at the memorial or funeral service in remembrance of one who has died

9. **extended metaphor**: a detailed or complex metaphor that is evident throughout a work

10. **foil**: a character who possesses traits that emphasize the characteristics and qualities of another character, either by being similar to or opposite from that character.

11. ★ **imagery**: language that appeals to the senses. Images are emotionally evocative. There are seven types of imagery: visual (sight), auditory (sound), tactile (touch), olfactory (smell), gustatory (taste), kinesthetic (movement), and organic (internal sense of being)

12. **invocation**: a prayer or a statement that calls for help from a god or goddess. *The Odyssey* begins with Homer's invocation: "Sing in me, muse, and through me tell the story. . ."

13. ★ **irony**: a discrepancy between appearance and reality. There are three types of irony: verbal (when what a character says is different from what he means); dramatic (when the reader knows something a character does not know); and situational (when something in the situation is incongruous with what may be expected).

14. ★ **metaphor**: a metaphor compares two generally dissimilar things (objects, places, ideas, etc.) in order to show something new or to help readers see something in a new way.

15. ★ **mood**: the dominant tone in a piece of literature; typically the emotional quality of the scene or setting

16. **motif**: a recurring element, an image or idea, in a work of literature, whose repetition emphasizes some aspect of the work (theme, plot, etc.)

17. **parable**: a short tale that teaches through example. Parables usually teach a moral or even religious lesson; they teach people about how they ought to live.

18. **paradox**: a situation or statement containing contradictory elements which nonetheless seem plausible or true

19. **parody**: a work of satire where the author imitates the language and form of another work to ridicule the author or work.

20. **soliloquy**: primarily found in Shakespeare's plays, a soliloquy is a monologue, one character on stage, or in the spotlight, who relates his/her plight. Hamlet's famous "To be or not to be" soliloquy is an example. Soliloquies are not meant to be heard by other characters.

21. **symbol**: a person, place, thing or idea that represents something else.

22. **syntax**: in general, the order of words in a sentence that results in various sentence types used for a variety of rhetorical effects (see Chapter 5)

23. ★ **tone**: the speaker or narrator's attitude towards something or the emotional quality of a passage (see Chapter 5)

24. **verisimilitude:** the quality in literature of being true to life; details seem realistic and believable, even if the setting is supernatural

25. **vernacular:** the ordinary, everyday speech of a region

It's difficult to understand literary elements out of context. As you read, identify various elements and make margin notes about their significance in the passage. See Chapter 10 on "Engaged and Active Reading."

BASIC ELEMENTS OF CLASSICAL TRAGEDY

1. **catharsis:** a purging of emotion, experienced by audiences especially through the pity they feel when witnessing the tragic hero's fall from grace

2. **chorus:** a group of characters in a play who comment on, but do not participate in, the action

3. **hamartia:** a tragic flaw; an unwitting error in judgment

4. **hubris:** excessive pride

5. **tragedy:** typically a drama in which a tragic hero experiences a fall from noble stature. The audience feels pity for the hero, but also fear that they, but for chance, could have been or might be in the hero's place.

6. **tragic hero:** a person of greater than normal stature (more noble, more attractive, smarter, etc.) who falls from grace (station of power, respect, or goodness) due to a tragic flaw (hamartia), or, more typically, pride (hubris)

Test Tip

If you have never read a Greek tragedy, begin with Oedipus Rex *or* Antigone, *both of which have been cited often on the AP Lit exam.*

TEN COMMON NOVEL TYPES

Note: Many books can be classified in more than one way.

1. **Bildungsroman (novel of education) or coming-of-age novel**: the protagonist is a child whose experiences teach him or her about the realities of the adult world. This transformation is often complex, painful, and filled with disillusionment.

2. **Dystopian novel**: presents readers with an apparent perfect (Utopian) society where human life is somehow diminished. Dark, prophetic themes: oppression, abuse of power, loss of individuality.

3. **Epistolary novel**: consists of letters written by one or more characters

4. **Gothic novel**: characterized by dark, mysterious setting; has supernatural elements, especially ghosts. Gothic novels tend to be highly emotional, even melodramatic.

5. **Historical novel**: story is immersed in historical events; characters interact with history.

6. **Novella**: prose fiction longer than a short story, but shorter than a novel.

7. **Novel of Manners**: the author details the social customs of an era and/or the social behaviors of a particular social group

8. **Picaresque novel**: an episodic novel (string of episodes or adventures) starring a picaro or rogue (a person of low social status) who wanders or has adventures.

9. **Social novel**: concerned with the effect of societal institutions and social conditions on humanity

10. **Utopian novel**: presents an ideal (perfect) society free from typical social problems

Basic Elements of Poetry

OVERVIEW

You will most likely read one or two poems in the multiple-choice section of the AP Lit exam and have one poem to analyze and write about in the essay section. Therefore, it is important to have a good background in poetry. Just as it is important to stretch your intellect by reading a wide variety of novels and plays, you should also push your limits by reading challenging poems. At the end of this chapter I have listed twenty "must read" poems. By listing these poems, I am not suggesting that they are the only poems you should read, but they are poems that are often anthologized, often studied in AP Lit courses, and they will provide you with a good beginning for your study of poetry.

One of the most difficult things for students to conceive of as they read poetry is how figurative language functions in a poem. Poems are, by their nature, full of figurative language: metaphor, simile, personification, and more. Reading beneath the surface is critical to understanding a poem. (See Chapter 10, "Engaged and Active Reading" for more help with reading a text closely.) Poetry begs to be read several times, and in your preparation for the AP Lit exam, you need to train yourself to diligently and carefully read complicated poems as well as prose pieces.

This chapter will acquaint you with the poetry terms and concepts you are most likely to encounter on the AP Lit exam.

WHAT IS A POEM MADE OF?

IMAGERY

Imagery is what occurs when poets use words that appeal to our senses: we perceive, through his or her words, an idea or image. These images can appeal to all senses: sight, hearing, touch, smell, and taste.

Imagery is important in a poem because it is language that allows us to be transported to another place, time, and experience, which, if the image is effective, allows us to understand the emotion being conveyed in the poem. Imagery is one of the main tools in creating a specific tone.

We can only know the world through the senses. We perceive first and reason second. Imagery is critical to understanding. Imagery allows the poet to show us meaning by taking us into the environment of the poem.

"Imagism" refers to the idea that an image, presented on its own, in a poem, has the power to unite the poet and the reader/listener in the exact impulse or experience that led the poet to write the poem in the first place.

DICTION

Diction is primarily the poet's choice of words. Since poetry, of all literary forms, uses the least number of words to accomplish its task, each word is important and must be chosen for its exactness. Also, unnecessary words should be eliminated so they don't obscure the essential language of the poem.

How does a poet choose the exact word? Three reasons make sense:

Sound: How does the word sound? Does the sound contribute to the meaning, to the overall sound scheme, or does it interrupt or interfere? See the section on sound for specific aspects of sound to consider.

Denotation: What is the exact meaning of the word? This is the definition you will find in the dictionary.

Connotation: What meanings does this word suggest beyond its exact meaning? What is the emotive quality of this word? For example, the word "cancer" means a disease characterized by the abnormal growth of cells. Emotionally, the word "cancer" conjures up fear, terror, worry, helplessness, etc. Words often have such connotative connections and we need to be aware of them when we use them.

Initially, most poets write the poem so they don't lose the impulse or the reason they wrote it in the first place. Then, after a time of "estrangement" from the poem, they go back and look critically at the poem, and at each word. Good poets know that each word matters. As a critical reader of poetry, students should never skim over any word in a poem.

SOUND

Poems are meant to be heard. It has been said that poetry is language the "drips from the tongue." We must pay attention to the sound of language as well as to the meaning of language. Sound, when used intentionally, should always enhance or reinforce meaning.

Sound elements:

Rhyme: words that sound either exactly alike or merely similar

Exact rhyme:

> ▸ cat, hat, flat, mat: *masculine rime (one syllable rhymes)*
>
> ▸ falling, calling, stalling: *feminine rime (two or more syllables rhyme)*

Slant rhyme/approximate rhyme:

> ▸ *the words sound close but are not exact rhymes*
>
> ▸ mirror, steer, dear *or* book, crack, stick *(consonance is used most often for slant rhymes).*

Internal rhyme vs. end rhyme: end rhyme occurs only at the end of the line whereas internal rhyme happens within the lines

Alliteration: repetition of beginning sounds in close proximity: "Susan sent sally some sunflowers," or "Loons lurk late in autumn lakes under lavender skies."

Assonance: repetition of vowel sounds: c*ake, stake, break, fate, drank, ache, placate,* etc. Some words using assonance will rhyme exactly: others will simply mirror the vowel sounds

Cacaphony: harsh, discordant, or unpleasing sounds

Consonance: repetition of consonant sounds: exact rhymes use consonance: *foot, put, soot.* But any words that repeat consonant sounds are using consonance: add suit, unfit, and unlit to the preceding list. The key is that they all end with the "t" sound. Consonance can occur in the middle of words also: *river, liver, cadaver, palaver, waver, save, rave,* etc. The "v" sound repeats.

Euphony: pleasing, melodious, pleasant sounds

Meter: a rhythm accomplished by using a certain number of beats or syllables per line: the most common form of meter is iambic meter which is a foot consisting of one unstressed syllable followed by a stressed syllable represented like this: (U /). A foot is simply two syllables (or in some cases, three) that form a metrical pattern. Iambs are common in everyday English. Iambic Pentameter means a five-foot Iambic line, or ten syllables.

Sound should never be more important than the idea or meaning of the poem, but should always work to extend the meaning of the poem.

Sound is less likely to be a significant factor in meaning in older, fixed form poems. Poets were not considered to have mastered their craft if they could not control rhyme schemes and metrical patterns. Free verse poets are free to experiment more liberally with sound, and for them, sound is something to mold, play with, and use to enhance their ideas.

METAPHOR

A metaphor is a comparison of two dissimilar things to help us see something in a new or more meaningful way. Similes are also metaphors, but use the words "like" or "as" in making the comparison. "Life is like a river" is a simile.

Besides the simile, there are two basic types of metaphor:

Direct metaphor: the comparison is made directly using the word "is." "Life is a river."

Indirect metaphor: "The river of life" also compares life to a river but does so indirectly.

Comparison is one of our basic patterns of reasoning. We perceive the world and compare new things/experiences to what we already know to see how they are alike or different and in this process, we make judgments and understand ideas.

There are other ways of comparing:

Personification: giving something non-human, human characteristics

Oxymoron: juxtaposing two things apparently contradictory that still reinforce one idea—jumbo shrimp, only choice, virtual reality

Hyperbole: using exaggeration to extend reality. Hyperbole gets us to look more closely at what is actually true by giving us a sharp contrast.

Understatement: this works in the opposite way from hyperbole. We use understatement when we say less than is appropriate for the situation or for our meaning.

THEME

Why write poems? Some people can't help it. Writing poetry is as natural to them as breathing and it's not a choice—they just do it. Still, there must be some reason beyond the process itself for writing poems. Theme is the purpose of the poem. It's what the poet needed to say. Themes express the unity of human experience, and through poems we see that we are more alike as a human race than different.

Themes tell us what is true about us, and they aren't always beautiful. Themes express the poet's vision—the artist's vision about the truth of the world. Some common themes are love, hate, hunger, growing up, growing old, dying, fears, cruelty, compassion, etc. A theme in a poem can be found in an epic tale or a simple reflection: both light the way to understanding.

SAYING SOMETHING NEW OR SAYING SOMETHING OLD IN A NEW WAY

Poetry is one of the oldest art forms, and poets have pretty much covered all there is to say. Still, we all are constantly reinventing ourselves and our world and we can say something new, or at least something old in a new way. As beginning poets, we learn, sometimes through imitating the great poems we admire. This is a good and natural way to learn. But we cannot imitate forever. At some point, we must find our own voices and we must allow them to say the things that "we know." "What you know that I don't know is what you can tell me in a poem," award-winning poet Sharon Olds said. "After all, what else is there? I cannot write about anything else. I can only tell you what I know."

This is a tricky thing, though. Sometimes we think we know things through our own experiences that we really don't—what we do is try to appropriate vicarious experience for our poems. Young poets may take a life lived on TV or in a movie and write about it as if it were their own. Ideas for poems can come through the observed lives of others—but what matters is what we know about that experience and this knowledge comes only from our own experience—from our own learning. This is what Olds meant: this is what we know.

Saying something old in a new way can mean using new forms, new ideas in language, infusing the truly new world of science/technology/reality with the very, very old questions of humanity. It's all about perception: how do you see the world? What can you say about it that hasn't already been said?

KEY TERMS

Familiarize yourself with the following list of terms. The starred terms (★) are those that have appeared more prominently on released AP Lit exams.

1. **alliteration:** repetition, at close intervals, of beginning sounds.

2. ★ **apostrophe**: a speaker directly addresses something or someone not living, as a lady in a tapestry, or the wind.

3. **assonance**: repetition at close intervals of vowel sounds. At its most basic, assonance is simple rhyme (cat, hat). Assonance provides a fluency of sound.

4. **consonance**: repetition at close intervals of consonant sounds, such as *book, plaque, thicker.*

5. **couplet**: two lines that rhyme. Shakespearean sonnets end with a couplet. Set off, couplets may contain a separate or complete idea. Sometimes a couplet can serve as a stanza.

6. ★ **epigram**: a short quotation or verse that precedes a poem (or any text) that sets a tone, provides a setting, or gives some other context for the poem.

7. **fixed form**: some poems have a fixed form, meaning that there are "rules" about numbers of lines, meter, rhyme schemes, etc. See a list of common fixed-form poems later in this chapter.

8. **iambic pentameter**: a line of five iambic feet, or ten syllables. See the section on Meter later in this chapter.

9. ★ **metaphor**: a comparison of two unlike things in order to show something new. A basic metaphor contains a literal term (the thing being compared) and a figurative term (the thing the literal term is being compared with).

10. ★ **imagery**: language that appeals to the senses and evokes emotion.

11. **metaphysical conceit**: an elaborate, intellectually ingenious metaphor that shows the poet's realm of knowledge; it may be brief or extended.

12. ★ **meter**: the rhythmic pattern of poetry. See the section on meter later in this chapter.

13. ★ **personification**: to personify is to attribute human qualities or characteristics to nonliving things. To attribute human qualities to animals is called **anthropomorphism**.

14. **pun**: a play on words where the juxtaposition of meanings is ironic or humorous.

15. **rhyme (internal rhyme)**: words that rhyme within a line of poetry

16. **rhyme (rhyme scheme)**: a regular pattern of end rhymes. To mark a rhyme scheme, label the first line "a," the next line if it does not rhyme with the first "b," and so on. Certain fixed form poems, like sonnets, have specific rhyme schemes.

17. **rhythm**: the beat or music of a poem. A regular beat indicates a metrical pattern.

18. **sestet**: a stanza of six lines. See other stanza types below.

19. **simile**: a metaphor that uses comparison words such as "like" or "as." An **epic simile** or **Homeric simile** (named after Homer) is an elaborate simile that compares an ordinary event or situation (familiar to the audience) with the idea in the text. These similes are often recognized by the "just as, so then" construction. Dante Alighieri makes extensive use of epic similes.

20. ★ **speaker**: the narrative voice of a poem. A poem generally has only one speaker, but some poems may have more than one.

21. ★ **stanza**: the "paragraph" of a poem, whether consisting of equal or unequal numbers of lines. **Stanzaic form** refers to a poem that has stanzas. A poem without stanzas is a **continuous form** poem.

22. ★ **structure**: the way the poem is built, such as three stanzas of terza rima, or one stanza (continuous form) of successive couplets

23. **synechdoche** (pronounced sin-**eck**-doe-key, emphasis on second syllable): the use of a part for the whole, such as "all hands on deck"

24. ★ **tone**: the emotional quality of a poem, such as regretful or contemplative. Tone also refers to the speaker's attitude (feelings about) a particular thing or idea.

25. **unity**: the degree to which elements of a poem work together to produce a coherent effect.

Remember to pay attention to stanza shifts. A new stanza may present a new idea or theme or a shift in tone.

HOW TO READ A POEM

As you read above, a poem is often full of figurative language, which means you shouldn't read a poem for its literal sense. You have to be open to surprises in poems. Good poets get us to feel before we think, and often we must read poems several times to get meaning from them.

It is possible to misread a poem. Sometimes students say that a poem can mean whatever you want it to mean, sort of like looking at an abstract painting and interpreting it however you like. However, you are not allowed to ignore the context of the poem when making your interpretation. A poem is a small thing, generally. Each word has been chosen carefully and it should have a purpose. You cannot simply notice some words and ignore others. If there is a word in a poem you don't understand, you have to look it up. This is different from reading a novel.

Below is a simple method of reading a poem. It will help you focus on what you should typically focus on so you can understand a complex poem.

1. **Read** the poem

   ▸ *Read slowly and, if possible, out loud.*

   ▸ *Read meaningful chunks, not lines. If there is punctuation, use it. If not, find discrete chunks of meaning (phrases and clauses).*

   ▸ *Be very careful of rhythmic poems that have a beat; you can lose your quest for meaning if you get caught up in the "music." However, the music might be a clue to the poet's theme, so keep it in mind.*

2. **Annotate** the poem for **STIFS** (see Chapter 10 for a sample annotated poem)

   S = Speaker

   ▸ *Identify the speaker and any particular character traits of the speaker (especially his or her point of view)*

   ▸ *Who is the speaker addressing?*

   ▸ *What is the speaker's topic, argument, etc.*

   T = Tone

   ▸ *What is the dominant tone in the poem?*

   ▸ *If so, where is it and why do you think the shift occurs?*

   I = Imagery

   ▸ *Isolate the major images: what do you see, smell, hear, taste, feel?*

   ▸ *What is suggested by the imagery? Emotion? Idea?*

F = Figurative Language

▸ *Find and understand the figurative language evident in the poem: metaphor, simile, apostrophe, personification, hyperbole, and more.*

▸ *Determine what's really being said in each example and how that relates to other elements in the poem.*

S = Sound

▸ *What sound elements are most striking and why? You should be looking for sound repetition, cacophony/euphony, or any element of sound that reinforces meaning.*

3. **Read** the poem again after you've annotated it.

4. If you are stuck on particular phrases, that is, if you don't understand them, make sure you have defined all complex language and then paraphrase the tricky parts. By simplifying the language in clauses and phrases, it will be easier for you to understand the basic idea.

5. **Answer this question:** What is this poem about and how do I know this? Be sure you can support your claims with evidence from the poem. Look to your annotations for your evidence. This question can serve as an essay prompt.

Test Tip

Understanding Shakespeare can be difficult. You might find it helpful to study smaller passages, such as sonnets, and paraphrase them until you get the knack of Elizabethan language.

METER

Meter is the regular pattern of accented and unaccented syllables in a poem.

There are generally very few questions on the AP Lit exam that ask you to determine meter, but if you have time, knowing about meter is good just in case there might be a question or two.

Meter is marked by stressed (/) and unstressed syllables (U). A metrical foot consists of either two syllables per foot (duple meter) or three syllables per foot (triple meter). The most common meter is iambic, a duple meter. The most common measure is iambic pentameter which is found throughout Shakespeare's works.

TYPES OF METER

Type	Adjective Form	Syllable pattern
iamb	iambic	U /
trochee	trochaic	/ U
anapest	anapestic	U U /
dactyl	dactylic	/ / U
spondee	spondaic	/ /

MEASURES OF METER

monometer	One foot
dimeter	Two feet
trimeter	Three feet

STANZA TYPES

couplet	two-line stanza
tercet	three-line stanza
quatrain	four-line stanza
quintain	five-line stanza
sestet	six-line stanza
septet	seven-line stanza
octave	eight-line stanza

COMMON FIXED FORM POEMS

Haiku: Haiku is a traditional Japanese fixed-form poem. It is structured in three lines, with five syllables in the first, seven syllables in the second, and five syllables in the third. One intention of a haiku poem is to capture a moment in time or a perceived aspect of nature.

Sestina: A sestina is a complicated French form of poetry traditionally consisting of six six-line stanzas followed by a tercet, called an "envoy," to equal 39 lines in all. A set of six words is repeated in varying patterns at the ends of the lines of each of the six-line stanzas. These six words also appear in the envoy, two in each line of the tercet.

Sonnet: You may have heard the phrase, "If it's square, it's a sonnet." A sonnet is fourteen lines of iambic pentameter, generally with either of two traditional rhyme schemes: Shakespearean/English: ABAB CDCD EFEF GG (three quatrains followed by a rhyming couplet); or Petrarchan/Italian: ABBAABBA CDECDE an octave (two quatrains) presenting a problem followed by a sestet (two tercets) giving the solution. Or, the sestet signals a change in tone or other shift.

Villanelle: This fixed-form poem consists of 19 lines composed of five tercets (rhyme scheme: aba) and a concluding quatrain (rhyme scheme: abaa). Lines one and three of the first tercet serve as refrains in a pattern that alternates through line 15. This pattern is repeated again in lines 18 and 19. The most famous example of a villanelle is Dylan Thomas' poem, *Do Not Go Gentle Into That Good Night*.

OTHER TYPES OF POEMS

1. **Ballad**: a short poem in song format (sometimes with refrains) that tells a story

2. **Elegy**: a poem, the subject of which is the death of a person or, in some cases, an idea

3. **Epic**: long, adventurous tale with a hero, generally on a quest

4. **Lyric**: expresses love, inner emotions, tends to be personal; usually written in first person

5. **Narrative**: the poet tells a story with characters and a plot

6. **Ode**: Originally a Greek form, odes are serious lyric poems. There are a variety of types of odes. English Romantic poets reinvigorated the form.

7. **Prose poem**: a prose poem looks like a paragraph, even having a jagged right margin. It may even read like a paragraph, but it retains poetic elements such as imagery, figurative language, and concise diction.

TWENTY "MUST READ" POEMS

There are thousands of great poems and hundreds of great poets. This list is meant only to acquaint you with some standard poems that AP Lit students often study. But please, do go beyond this list. Embrace poems and they will cease to frighten you. The following poems are in no particular order. They are examples of old, new, British, and American poems. Each one should be easy to find in a good college literature anthology, and many may even be online.

1. *My Last Duchess*, Robert Browning

2. *The Lovesong of J. Alfred Prufrock*, T.S. Eliot

3. *Ozymandias*, Percy Bysshe Shelley

4. *A Valediction: Forbidding Mourning*, John Donne (or anything by Donne)

5. *Out, Out—*, Robert Frost

6. *Dover Beach*, Matthew Arnold

7. *Bells for John Whiteside's Daughter*, John Crowe Ransom

8. *The Second Coming*, William Butler Yeats

9. *Dulce et Decorum Est,* Wilfred Owen

10. *I felt a Funeral, in my Brain,* Emily Dickinson

11. *Those Winter Sundays*, Robert Hayden

12. *To His Coy Mistress*, Andrew Marvell

13. *The Weary Blues*, Langston Hughes

14. *Woman Work*, Maya Angelou

15. *Do Not Go Gentle Into That Good Night*, Dylan Thomas

16. *In the Waiting Room,* Elizabeth Bishop

17. *Ode on a Grecian Urn,* John Keats

18. *Sunday Morning,* Wallace Stevens

19. *The Colonel,* Carolyn Forché

20. Any Shakespearean sonnet

Basic Elements of Language

OVERVIEW

This chapter has two main purposes. The first is to fill in the gaps in terminology between fiction/drama and poetry. There are certain terms that are vital to all areas of writing. The term "metaphor" is one of them. But there are other terms that are more specific to a genre or purpose, such as rhyme scheme for poetry or soliloquy for drama. This chapter aims to define more terms that you may need to know for the exam.

The second purpose of this chapter is to give you a basic understanding of rhetoric and why it is important on the AP Lit exam. The AP English Language and Composition exam is the full-fledged test of your rhetorical skills, but there are some questions on the AP English Literature and Composition exam that have to do with argument and persuasion. The terms and concepts in this chapter focus on the uses of language, aspects of argument, and elements of linguistic style.

WHAT IS RHETORIC?

Rhetoric is the use of language to persuade. In more general terms, rhetoric is the effective use of language for a variety of purposes. If you intend to study for the AP English Language and Composition exam, you will become much more intimately familiar with rhetoric and rhetorical devices. For now, though, it is enough to recognize a few basic aspects.

You may be presented with an argument in a variety of genres: essay, poem, narrative prose, even an excerpt from a novel. For example, a poet may argue that time is short, so it is best to love while we can, as in Marvell's poem *To His Coy Mistress*. Marvell's poem is an excellent example of a highly structured argument in poetic form.

A variety of questions regarding rhetoric are typically found on the AP Lit exam. Some common types are listed below:

- The question asks you to determine the primary rhetorical effect, purpose, or function of a passage or section.

- The question asks you to identify the central rhetorical strategy used in the passage. See more on rhetorical strategies below.

- The question asks you to determine the purpose, function, or rhetorical purpose of a sentence, phrase, clause, or word.

- The question asks you to determine the effect of a rhetorical shift.

KEY TERMS

1. **abstraction**: a concept or idea without a specific example; idealized generalities

2. **abstract noun**: ideas or things that can mean many things to many people, such as peace, honor, etc.

3. **analogy**: compares two things that are similar in several respects in order to prove a point or clarify an idea

4. **antecedent**: that which comes before; the antecedent of a pronoun is the noun to which the pronoun refers (you may be expected to find this relationship)

5. **antithesis**: the opposite of an idea used to emphasize a point; the juxtaposition of contrasting words or ideas. Example: *To err is human; to forgive, divine.*

6. **catalog (list)**: Walt Whitman used catalogs or lists of like elements in his poems; lists of details can reinforce a concept. Inductive arguments build to a conclusion based on the collective impression of lists (facts).

7. **circumlocution**: to write around a subject; to write evasively; to say nothing

8. **double entendre**: a phrase or saying that has two meanings, one being sexual or provocative in nature

9. **euphemism**: a kinder, gentler, less crude or harsh word or phrase to replace one that seems imprudent to use in a particular situation

10. **ethos**: a speaker or writer's credibility; his or her character, honesty, commitment to the writing

11. **hyperbole**: an exaggeration or overstatement—saying more than is warranted by the situation in order to expose reality by comparison; also, one of the main techniques in satire

12. **juxtapose (juxtaposition)**: to place side by side in order to show similarities or differences

13. **lists**: see catalog

14. **oxymoron**: a figure of speech in which two contradictory elements are combined for effect, such as "deafening silence"

15. **paradox**: the juxtaposition of incongruous or conflicting ideas that reveal a truth or insight

16. **parody**: a humorous imitation of an original text meant to ridicule, used as a technique in satire

17. **parallel structure**: equal or similar grammatical or rhetorical elements used side by side or in succession, generally for emphasis

18. **pathos**: the quality in literature that appeals to the audience's emotions

19. **repetition**: any of a variety of devices that emphasize through repetition: one example of a repetition device is *anaphora*, which is the repetition of the same word or words at the beginning of successive phrases, clauses, or sentences

20. **rhetoric**: the use of language for persuasion (in our context, persuasive writing)

21. **rhetorical strategy**: various strategies and appeals that writers use to persuade. The main appeals are to logic/reason, to needs, to tradition, to emotion, and to ethics/fairness.

22. **satire**: type of literature that exposes idiocy, corruption, or other human folly through humor, exaggeration, and irony

23. **understatement**: saying less than is warranted by the situation in order to emphasize reality

24. **verb phrase:** the verb and its object and modifiers

25. **vernacular**: the ordinary, everyday speech of a region

BASIC RHETORICAL STRATEGIES

Entire books have been written on this subject, but you don't have the time or the need to read one of those. Instead, know these basic strategies and you will do well.

BASIC APPEALS:

A writer can appeal to readers'

- **needs** (hierarchy of needs: shelter, esteem, etc.)

- **sense of tradition** (we've always done it this way)

- **ethics** (sense of fairness, right or wrong)

- **emotions** (pull at the heartstrings)

- **logic/reason** (suggest what is logical and support it with a reasoned argument)

There are also appeals to

- **authority** (stating facts, expert opinion, statistics)

- **accepted values** (success, freedom, equality, etc.)

STYLISTIC DEVICES EFFECTIVE WRITERS USE:

- evocative or emotive language
- lists of relevant details
- figurative language, especially to get readers to see things in a fresh way
- imagery, appeals to senses and draws readers in to the text
- repetition, used for emphasis
- parallel structure, used for emphasis
- irony, gets us to see the truth
- analogy, shows logical relationships

MODES/FORMS OF RHETORIC

- cause and effect
- problem and solution
- narrative
- description
- definition
- humor
- satire

THE VERBS OF RHETORIC

The questions and prompts in the AP Lit exam are loaded with a variety of verbs. It is important to know what each means, as subtle differences may be important in understanding the question or your task.

Allege: to assert but without proof; allegations require proof

Analyze: to break apart; to look at component parts of a text in order to understand an aspect of the whole

Argue: to defend a claim, to provide evidence for an assertion

Assert: to formally declare as true

Broach: to bring up a topic for discussion

Characterize: to depict something in a certain way; to give specific characteristics of someone or something

Claim: to make a statement of "fact," something you intend to prove.

Clarify: to draw distinctions, to make more evident, to lessen confusion

Discuss: to consider in writing a variety of possible views (ways of interpretation) on a topic

Dramatize: to give a story to a situation, to add vivid details, such as imagery, figurative language, etc.

Emphasize: to give added importance or weight to something

Establish: to set a foundation for, to base a claim on an observation

Imply: to state indirectly; to have a logical consequence

Indicate: to be a signal of; to state or express

Observe: to take notice of, and thereby, it is implied, to draw conclusions.

Paraphrase: to put into more common, less complex (or technical) language

Propose: to suggest a plan or a solution to a problem

Rebuff: to reject

Suggest: to offer a perspective, a solution, a way of thinking about something for consideration

Support: to give reasons and examples for a statement of fact or a claim.

A QUESTION OF GRAMMAR

The AP Lit exam is not a grammar test. It is a literary analysis test. However, your ability to control the conventions of good writing is expected. Also, there tend to be a few questions that ask about relationships between words or parts of sentences. These types of questions test your ability to read and comprehend complex poetry and prose.

Examples:

1. The question asks you to identify what a phrase or clause modifies.

2. The question asks you to make a grammatical connection, such as "The word or phrase refers to . . ."

3. The question asks you to find a word's antecedent.

Hopefully, none of the terms in the preceding questions trouble you, but if so, here are some definitions.

PHRASE:

- A phrase is a group of related words that does not contain a subject and verb. There are a variety of phrase types, but it is unlikely that you will be asked to identify phrase types.

CLAUSE:

- An independent clause is also called a main clause or, more commonly, a sentence. An independent clause has a subject and a verb and can stand independently.

- A subordinate or dependent clause has either a subject or a verb and cannot stand independently.

MODIFIES:

- *Modifies* means to add meaning to, such as adjectives modifying nouns (*blue* dress) or adverbs modifying verbs (walked *slowly*)

ANTECEDENT:

- *Antecedent* means that which comes before. Pronouns have antecedents. "Laura found her hat on the top shelf." Laura is the antecedent of the pronoun her.

The AP Lit exam also tests your ability to write complex or sophisticated prose when writing your essays. When you write, you'll need to consider the types of sentences and how you vary them, the vocabulary you use, including the kinds of verbs you use, and much more. See Chapter 15 for tips on writing well.

Mastering Difficult Vocabulary

"Too many students do not possess the vocabulary and do not understand the various nuances of language to be able to read imaginative literature."

—The College Board

OVERVIEW

The following words were chosen from AP Lit released exams because they are generally difficult, may be archaic in meaning or have a specific cultural meaning.

The purpose of this list is not to imply that these words will show up on future exams, but to suggest that in order for you to confidently deal with complex texts, you need to have a fairly extensive vocabulary, not just words you know the meanings of, but words you are comfortable using in a variety of contexts.

VOCABULARY LIST

1. adamantine (adj): (from the noun adamant, which is a hard, crystallized carbon) firm in attitude or opinion, unyielding (contemporary usage: adamant, meaning firm, unyielding)

2. admonish (verb): to scold, censor

3. amorphous (adj): without shape or form

4. animal husbandry (noun): the practice of breeding and raising livestock (also called animal science)

5. apostles (noun): the 12 men who were Jesus's "entourage"

6. austere (adj)/austerity (noun): severe or stern in disposition or appearance, having great self denial (materialistically)

7. bade (verb): to order, to instruct

8. belies (verb): contradicts

9. bellicose (adj): loud, argumentative, prone to fighting

10. benign (adj): harmless

11. bosom (noun): the chest, typically a woman's and place of warmth and love

12. chaste (adj): pure, virginal

13. **chasten** (verb): to chastise, castigate, correct

14. **couch, couched** (verb): to word in a certain manner

15. **cultivate** (verb): to grow, to nurture

16. **curate, curates:** (noun): a clergyman; (verb): to direct or manage a museum or an exhibit

17. **damask** (noun): a fabric of linen or cotton or silk or wool with a reversible pattern woven into it

18. **degenerate** (verb): to degrade or lessen in value; (noun): a morally bankrupt person, a profligate

19. **deity** (noun): a god

20. **din** (noun): loud, raucous noise

21. **dumb** (adj): mute, unable to speak

22. **effeminate** (adj): having feminine qualities, generally only used to describe men

23. **eminent** (adj)/**eminence** (noun): distinguished, having high stature

24. **emulate** (verb): to imitate or copy (as with a role model)

25. **entreat** (verb)/**entreaty** (noun): to beg/begging

26. **equinox** (noun): either of two times of the year when the sun crosses the plane of the earth's equator and day and night are of equal length

27. **facility** (noun)/**facile** (adj): adeptness/with ease

28. **faculty** (noun): ability, power

29. **homage** (noun): respect, honor

30. **hutch** (noun): a cupboard for dishes or rabbits

31. **impervious** (adj): not able to be penetrated

32. impious (adj): irreverent

33. indefatigable (adj): inability to tire, tireless

34. indict (verb)/indictment (noun): to charge, to accuse/a charge or accusation

35. inherent (adj)/inherently (adverb): integral, intrinsic/in an inherent manner

36. jocund (adj): merry, mirthful, gay

37. languor (noun): state of ease, rest, even listlessness

38. lentils (noun): small split pea-like legume

39. lethargic (adj): tired, listless

40. lore (noun): traditional knowledge, passed on through fables, stories, etc.

41. mien (noun): bearing, presence, manner

42. naivete (noun)/naïve (adj): innocence, inexperience

43. nascent (adj): emerging, newly born or created

44. ordain (verb): to appoint to a clerical post (minister, priest) or to order due to superior authority

45. parody (verb or noun): to spoof, to mock; a parody is a text meant to spoof or mock (a form of satire)

46. phenomenon (noun): a remarkable development

47. piety (noun): righteousness, godliness

48. plight (noun): predicament, quandary, difficulty

49. pretense (noun): deception, deceit

50. primeval (adj): aboriginal, primordial, primal (first)

51. prodigy (noun): genius, especially a gifted child

52. proffer (verb): to suggest, to propose

53. profundity (noun): intellectual depth; penetrating knowledge; keen insight; etc

54. promulgate (verb): to proclaim or exclaim

55. prowess (noun): special skill

56. quarry (noun): prey, victim; also a pit where gravel or ore is mined

57. raiment (noun): especially fine or decorative clothing

58. reap (verb): to gather, glean, harvest

59. reticent (adj)/reticence (noun): shyness, unwillingness

60. rheumatism (noun): painful disorder of the joints or muscles or connective tissues

61. sable (noun): as a color, dark, black-brown, fur from the animal sable

62. scourge (noun): bane, curse, affliction or a whip, lash, punishment

63. sepulcher (noun): burial chamber, tomb

64. sire (noun and verb): a father; to father, engender

65. supine (adj): lying prone, flat, especially in humility

66. suppliant (verb and noun): to petition or beseech, one who begs for intercession

67. surplice (noun): a loose-fitting white ecclesiastical vestment with wide sleeves

68. temper, tempered (verb): toughen (steel or glass) by a process of gradually heating and cooling

69. timorous (adj): timid, fearful, apprehensive

70. tinged (adj): slightly touched with

71. tumult (noun): tumultuous (adj): uproar, disturbance

72. **vehement (adj)/vehemence (noun):** marked by extreme intensity of emotions or convictions; inclined to react violently

73. **veracity (noun):** truthfulness

74. **vocation (noun):** a calling, such as the ministry; a job one seems meant to do.

75. **Whorl (noun):** swirl, ringlet, curlicue

Make learning new words a game. When you learn a new word, commit to using it at least ten times in one day in a variety of contexts. Bonus: You might have fun annoying those around you!

MY OWN VOCABULARY LIST

In Chapter 10, Engaged and Active Reading, you are encouraged to annotate texts as you read and circle words that you don't know. You may want to add those words here, and look them up to help you increase your working vocabulary.

Word	Definition
1.	
2.	
3.	
4.	
5.	
6.	
7.	
8.	
9.	
10.	
11.	
12.	
13.	
14.	
15.	
16.	
17.	
18.	
19.	
20.	

PART III:

INTERPRETING READING PASSAGES

Engaged and Active Reading

IMPROVING READING HABITS

In the multiple-choice section of the AP Lit exam, you will have 60 minutes to carefully read five to six texts, a combination of fictional prose, essay, and poetry and answer approximately 55 questions on those texts (see Chapter 19). In the essay section, you will have two texts to read—generally a poem and a prose passage. If you don't understand what you've read, you will not be able to write intelligent essays.

In either case, you will not have time for leisurely reading. However, you still must be able to read actively and reflectively with all your faculties engaged. You may only have time to read each text once, so you need to read carefully and with purpose.

You know your reading habits need some improvement if any of the following is true for you:

- you find yourself thinking of something else about every other sentence

- you have to reread a paragraph about five times to know what it means

- you have to look up about every other word

- you are bored by the passage so you just skim through it, but then you have no idea what it is about

- you sometimes characterize the text as "stupid," "dumb," "pointless," etc.

Some of the problems listed above have to do with **your attitude** about the reading. It is fair to say that not all the passages and poems on the AP Lit exam will be to your liking, but it will be important for you to control your negative emotional response. Negative emotions will interfere with your motivation and will cloud your ability to think clearly. The fix? Approach each passage as something you can mostly understand. You aren't expected to be an expert on any of them.

If you find yourself rereading a lot, you may actually be reading too slowly—allowing outside thoughts into your head. This is a matter of **concentration** and it is something you can control. Before exam day, practice reading complex texts at a rate faster than you would normally read—not so fast that you are skimming the text—but quickly enough to concentrate on the text and to keep those outside thoughts at bay. Remember, you do not have to read every single word in a prose passage to know what the author is saying.

MORE STRATEGIES FOR IMPROVING YOUR READING

- Make a conscious effort to understand what you're doing as you read. As soon as your mind starts wandering, toss out a mental lasso and pull yourself back. Work on keeping your focus.

- If you start to get tired, drink water, not energy drinks, and remember to breathe. Do some neck exercises to get your blood circulating to your brain. You won't be allowed to get up and walk around during the exam, so try to get used to reading, concentrating, and thinking for periods of an hour or more at a time.

- Let your body help you read. Your text should be in line with your sight. Your visual path can't bend. Prop up your book—don't lay it flat on a desk or table. And your arms will get tired if you try to hold a book up while lying flat on the floor or in bed. Practice your reading while sitting at a desk or a table, as this is the most likely position you'll be in while taking the AP exam.

- Minimize distractions. Do NOT read while listening to music on your mp3 player! You may think you are concentrating, but, in reality, you are forcing your brain to think of two things at once, a practice that is stressful and counter-productive for exam prep. You will not be allowed to have any electronic devices with you for the exam, so get used to reading in relative silence.

- Practice controlling your emotions by choosing some tough texts to read. Read them, annotate them, and feel good about your progress. Read Shakespeare, Jane Austen, Voltaire, or Dostoevsky, to start. A lot of older texts are online. You can download them to an e-reader, or read them online. If you really want to practice annotating the text, it is best to have hard copies of the texts. You can search Project Gutenberg (http://www.gutenberg.org), for example, to find many of the authors listed in Chapters 3 and 4.

- Give yourself permission to skip words. You don't have to read every single word to know what's going on. This is not to say that you should skim—not at all, but if you think you have to look up every word, you will miss the "big picture." This is especially true of novels, plays, or longer works. In short poems, each word is going to more important just because there are so few of them to begin with.

- Learn how annotate texts and practice this skill before the exam. This may be the most important thing you can do to improve your reading skills for the AP Lit exam. There is more on this later in this chapter.

- When you take your AP Lit exam, plan to quickly skim the multiple-choice questions that relate to a text. You won't have time to read all of the questions first, but if you know there is a question on mood and another on irony, you can look for those aspects in the text and mark them as you read.

Test Tip

Be a reading Ninja! Think of each text on the exam as a noble, worthy opponent, but one that will not defeat you. Respect these literary opponents, recognize their strengths and special elements, but feel confident that you can read, understand, and respond to them. Never think you are too weak for any reading challenge!

ANNOTATING A TEXT

WHY ANNOTATE

When you read a difficult text, you're not usually reading for pleasure. You want to understand the text and you want to read it as quickly as possible (especially on the AP Lit exam). Difficult texts are not easy to understand quickly, so annotating or marking the text as you read can help you grasp the key ideas and help you more easily reconnect with your thoughts when you take a second look.

For example, if you are reading a poem and immediately recognize the dominant tone—mark that down. If the tone shifts in the last stanza—note that as well. If a question that follows the passage asks you to identify the tone, you'll most likely be able to answer it without rereading the text—all because you annotated!

HOW TO ANNOTATE

Earlier in this book, you were given a list of key literary elements to know so you would recognize them in prose and poems. Your knowledge of literary elements will make it much easier for you to spot significant details in texts. The other part of marking a text is knowing what to look for.

Annotating or marking a text means that as you read you underline key words, mark key phrases or ideas and make margin notes. This process facilitates active and engaged reading. If you are making notes while you read, if you are actively looking for what to mark, you will be less likely to drift off and to start thinking about something else. You are also training yourself to recognize the most significant literary aspects of a poem or prose passage.

As you read, keep the elements of style in mind—diction, imagery, tone, syntax, point of view, and figurative language (see Chapter 5).

PRACTICE ANNOTATING

Start practicing your annotating skills **now**, so you can train yourself. At first, practicing this skill may cause your reading speed to slow down. But, with time and practice, you'll be back to reading quickly and more deeply at the same time.

As you are learning this skill, practice annotating nearly everything you read. When you read, always have a pen or pencil in hand, even if you are reading a magazine. Once you've mastered the skills you'll annotate only the texts you wish to study. Annotating is not something you would do for pleasure reading, unless your pleasure is to read and understand difficult books. If so, read with a pen in hand.

On the AP Lit exam, definitely annotate the texts. Use your annotating skills on the passages and poems in both the multiple-choice and free-response sections.

Once you've mastered your annotating skills, they'll serve you well for any analytical reading you do. You will have developed a reading skill that will help you read and study all kinds of texts in college and beyond, not just literary works.

Practice, practice, practice!

SUGGESTED SYMBOLS FOR ANNOTATING

Whether you use the suggested symbols below or create your own, it is important to keep it simple (use only a few symbols) and stay consistent.

(oval/ellipse shape)	Circle unfamiliar words. You won't be allowed to use a dictionary on the AP Lit exam, but just circling unfamiliar words reminds you to try to understand them by using context clues. When you do have a dictionary available, look up the word if you cannot fully grasp its meaning from the context. Add these unfamiliar words to your list of words (see Chapter 9).
————	Underline words in close proximity that share connotative or denotative associations.
!	An exclamation point in the margin near a group of lines indicates a key idea; pair with brackets around specific text
?	A question mark in the margin means "I don't understand." Noting questions prompts you to answer them later.
text	Write brief notes in the margins to make your thinking visually accessible and easy to connect with when you take a second look at the text. Your notes can be about anything, but should include conclusions you've drawn about the text so far.
[ ]	Use brackets around phrases or chunks of text (or enclose in a rectangle) to mark significant literary elements, such as symbols, motifs (keep a count also), figurative language, etc. Label the element in the margin. Make corresponding notes about what these might mean. For example, don't simply mark that water is a symbol, but write a note about it being a symbol for purity that reinforces the innocence of the main character.

SAMPLE ANNOTATED TEXTS

The prose passage below is from Willa Cather's novel *My Antonia*. The poem is John Donne's *The Broken Heart*. These samples are meant to give you an idea of what an annotated text looks like. As you study each one, you may find other literary elements that you would have marked or made note of. If so, it shows you are thinking critically. Good for you!!

Try writing an essay for each of the texts below using the insights in the annotations. Use this generic prompt to guide you: *What is the narrator's/speaker's attitude toward the setting/situation?*

Excerpt from *My Antonia* by Willa Cather

Jim Burden is narrating this passage.

[annotation: 1st person narrator]

I sat down in the middle of the garden, where snakes could
scarcely approach unseen, and leaned my back against a warm
yellow pumpkin. There were some ground-cherry bushes growing
along the furrows, full of fruit. I turned back the papery triangular
sheaths that protected the berries and ate a few. All about me giant
grasshoppers, twice as big as any I had ever seen, were doing
acrobatic feats among the dried vines. The gophers scurried up and
down the ploughed ground. There in the sheltered draw-bottom the
wind did not blow very hard, but I could hear it singing its
humming tune up on the level, and I could see the tall grasses
wave. The earth was warm under me, and warm as I crumbled it
through my fingers. Queer little red bugs came out and moved in
slow squadrons around me. Their backs were polished vermilion,
with black spots. I kept as still as I could. Nothing happened. I did
not expect anything to happen. I was something that lay under the
sun and felt it, like the pumpkins, and I did not want to be anything
more. I was entirely happy. Perhaps we feel like that when we die
and become a part of something entire, whether it is sun and air, or
goodness and knowledge. At any rate, that is happiness; to be
dissolved into something complete and great. When it comes to
one, it comes as naturally as sleep.

[handwritten annotations:]

Overall tone:
Contentment / contented
tone.

* he's safe — he nestles into nature.

sustenance

entertaining place

Jim contemplates one of the big questions: What happens to us when we die?

Colors:
warm reds & yellows & oranges reinforce warm feeling.
Sun - yellow, too.

< tactile imagery

He's one among them and he respects their movement an life. He won't scare the red bugs. He's also part of something bigger. Pantheism?

What is happiness but contentment?

The contentment of the day extends to something more universal: the contentment of death, esp. if one dissolves "into something complete & great."

Life on earth is fully sustaining and we belong there as do pumpkins. But life beyond earth is also fully sustaining & where we belong.

What does it mean to be happy?

Not to fear - to welcome.

Movement:
grasshoppers "doing acrobatic feats"
"gophers scurried"
"tall grasses wave"
Jim crumbles the earth through his fingers
bugs move in slow squadrons
Even the wind is active & singing
Our movement = our purpose
Action = Life   We also move from life to death.

Diction:

"Decay"–"devour"–
"plague"–"burn") Suggest death, end of being.

The Broken Heart

Speaker is addressing a former love who broke his heart.

He is stark mad, who ever says, [crazy]
  That he hath been in love an hour,)
Yet not that love so soon decays,
  But that it can ten in less space devour;
Who will believe me, if I swear
That I have had the plague a year? — love sickness – or been in love.
  Who would not laugh at me, if I should say,
  I saw a flask of powder burn a day?

Love doesn't last. Anyone who's really been in love knows this.

Metaphor – Love is compared to the pike –

Ah, what a trifle is a heart, meaningless
  If once into love's hands it come!
All other griefs allow a part
  To other griefs, and ask themselves but some;
They come to us, but us Love draws,
He swallows us, and never chaws:) eats us whole – just gulps.
  By him, as by chain'd shot, whole ranks do die,
He is the tyrant pike, our hearts the fry.

Love eats us alive as if we're nothing of value.

other griefs leave us something to feel.

Love is a grief, but a greedy one.

proof (

Love personified – a voracious eater.

Love is the big fish ① and our hearts are the little fish ② that the big fish eats.

If 'twere not so, what did become ②
  Of my heart, when I first saw thee?)
I brought a heart into the room,
  But from the room, I carried none with me:
If it had gone to thee, I know
Mine would have taught thine heart to show
  More pity unto me: but Love, alas,
  At one first blow did shiver it as glass.

If my heart had gone to you – it would have taught you to have pity on me.)

Love at first sight.

implies her heart was cruel.

when I first saw you I lost my heart.

shatter in shards like glass

Yet nothing can to nothing fall,
  Nor any place be empty quite,)
Therefore I think my breast hath all one ②
  Those pieces still, though they be not unite;
And now as broken glasses show mirrors (mini reflections)
  A hundred lesser faces, so
My rags of heart can like, wish, and adore, torn/shredded
  But after one such love, can love no more.
                                   (you)

But it is not logical that my breast is empty – so I must still have my heart although in "a million" pieces – all too small to reflect or love again.

—John Donne

Metaphor – Comparing broken heart to broken mirror.

Negative tone his heart is ruined for love

Shattered glass cannot be mended.

After having loved you – my heart can no longer love. You broke my heart & ruined me for others.

Understanding Literary Analysis

". . . memorizing the name of a technique or being able to identify a technique is only the first step in analysis. The final step is to explain *how* a technique contributes to meaning," says the College Board in Student Performance Questions and Answers: 2008 AP English Literature and Composition Free-Response Questions.

In This Chapter

Overview

It Is Possible . . .

Controlling Your Biases

Typical Problems

Generating Your Analysis

CSE: A Formula to Remember

OVERVIEW

Analysis means to take apart and examine component parts of a whole in order to gain a greater understanding of the whole. The AP Lit exam gives you two opportunities to show your analysis skills. First, in the multiple-choice section, typically you'll read, analyze, and respond to questions on several prose passages and two poems. Secondly, the free-response section is where you will show that you can read a complex passage, generate a defensible thesis, and argue that thesis in a well-organized essay.

Generally when we read a scholarly work and are expected to analyze and interpret our reading, we are given time. We sometimes work with others through discussion to sort out our reactions. A written analysis goes through several drafts. However, the AP Lit exam puts your skills to a rigorous test by expecting lucid, insightful analysis in a very short time span—about three hours. The purpose of this chapter is to suggest ways for you to maximize your interpretative and analytical skills.

IT IS POSSIBLE . . .

1. to misread the passage

2. to be arguing the wrong thing

3. to write about nothing

4. to choose the exact wrong word

5. to fail to answer the question

CONTROLLING YOUR BIASES

One of the main impediments to improving your skills is to think that you already know everything you need to know. It is far better to keep an open mind and to engage with a critical eye your own reading and writing processes, knowing that you can get better rather than to rely on what you've known in the past.

Perhaps the biggest obstacle for teens who are struggling to understand complex literary texts is their lack of life and world experience. There is only so much one can know at age 17 or 18!

We all have biases. They come from particular aspects of our lives that influence how we think. Biases are not wrong, but they can limit our ability to think with an open mind. This section is simply asking that you consider this important part of your thinking process and understand how biases can limit your ability to not only read and understand a poem or prose passage, but also limit your ability to write about it.

To avoid problems with biases, consider the following:

1. Watch for **undue sympathy,** which tends to emerge from immature readers. For example, Wilbur's poem "Death of a Toad," presents the last stages of a toad's life. Students who can't get past the gross-out factor will be stuck there and will not be able to see the toad as an important actor in life's great pageant. Similarly, those who focus on the blood-stained sheet and feel only sympathy for the dead wolf in McCarthy's passage from *The Crossing* might miss the fact that it is the young man we need to understand, not the wolf. To stay on track in a situation like this, focus on the prompt and the task it presents. Do not stray into emotional realms that are unrelated to your task.

2. Accept that you have **values and views** that might be particular and not universal. One's religious faith, ethnic heritage, political persuasion, or local social values, for example, sometimes limit one's ability to understand a text. It is not fair to expect a literary text to conform to your standards. The text is as it is. It is not wrong. It is not right. It is a text. To simplify: Do not judge the morality of a character unless that is the intent of the passage and indicated in the prompt.

3. Our **place in time** can be an impediment to our understanding. While it may be true that people of all times are more alike than different, social and cultural aspects do impact people. People who live in the age of technology have different concerns than those who lived prior to the industrial revolution. Applying the parameters of one's own time to all time is not wise. For example, never make uniformed blanket statements about the past, such as, "In the old days, people's lives were simpler." A good understanding of history will help you avoid such misstatements.

4. One limitation of immature readers is that they tend to see everything only through their **own experience**. If you've ever had a conversation with anyone who, instead of listening to what you have to say, jumps in with, "Oh, I know. That happened to me, too." and turns the focus to him or herself, you know what I mean. The experience or situation revealed in the poem or prose passage may indeed make you think about your own experience. And that is good because we don't really understand things we can't connect with. However, once you start formulating your thesis and working through your analysis, you must focus on the text. Your deep understanding of a passage or poem comes from the wisdom of your experience. However, the proof of your thesis must come from the text and not your experience.

TYPICAL PROBLEMS

This list of literary analysis problems comes from comments made by AP Lit readers about lower-scored essays. Be sure to pay attention to the suggested solutions or strategies.

A: I READ AND UNDERSTOOD THE TEXT. WHY DID I GET A LOW SCORE?

Even if you have read the passage correctly and you've accurately grasped the main point of the text, you still may fail in your analysis if you have any of the problems listed below:

Problem *The writer . . .*	*Solution/Strategy*
Fails to support claims with textual evidence.	You cannot simply state claims without proving them. If your reader constantly needs proof, you have not done your job. If you say something is so, then you have to show how it is so by citing your proof from the text.
Relies on only one or two claims and simply repeats those again and again.	Even if the points are excellent, repeating them again and again shows you don't really have anything else in your bag of tricks. If you find yourself relying on one or two claims, go back to the text. What did you miss?
Provides too little analysis.	The writer doesn't go far enough. Some students are happy with a minimum effort. This attitude will not help you earn a high score. You should never just say, "good enough."

Continued →

(Continued from previous page)

Problem The writer . . .	Solution/Strategy
Is disorganized. His/her points are disconnected, illogically place and inconsistently argued.	Disorganization seems to be the result of not having thought your essay out at the beginning. It is important to make a mini-outline in the margin of your page. While you may not follow it exactly, this outline will help you reconnect to thoughts you had and points you wanted to make. It should also help you avoid digression. Find a good list of transitional words and phrases and learn to integrate them naturally into your writing. This will help you with organization.
Has too many errors, such as blatant misspellings (author's name, title, character's etc.)	If a word is in the prompt or the passage, there is no excuse for misspelling it. Simply give a visual backward glance before proceeding. Misspelling easy words is not good for AP-level students. Be careful. If you're using a difficult word, one you can use fluently when you speak, but you simply forget how to spell it, put a little "(sp.)" behind it, indicating that you forgot. It's one thing to misspell "ignominious" and another to write "metafor." You simply must know how to write complete and fluent sentences and punctuate them. See Chapter 15 for more help with this.

Problem *The writer . . .*	*Solution/Strategy*
Does not explain why or show how his/her claim is true.	Stating a claim and giving proof from the text is only part of your job as a writer. You need to explain what you mean. You need to show how or why what you say is true. Many times students think an idea is self evident, so they leave it to explain itself. This is a poor strategy. Find sample essays that have been given high scores and analyze how those students develop their thinking with solid explanations.
Has too many claims.	If you have too many claims in support of your thesis, your analysis is most likely going to be superficial. It is best to settle on several significant aspects of the text, rather than point out every little thing. Your essay is not to be a frenzied show of how much you noticed, but instead, it should show your ability to distinguish between meaningless and truly arguable claims and between those that are, while true, somewhat flat in their relevance. If you have six claims you can argue, pick the best three or four. Depth, not breadth, is what is called for.

B: YOU'VE MISREAD PART OR ALL OF THE TEXT.

Problem *The writer . . .*	*Solution/Strategy*
Relies on paraphrase or summary.	This is what happens when you don't understand what you've read. If you don't really get the point of what you've read, but you know you've got to write something, you tend to simply restate the text or summarize it. If you do this, your score will be quite low. Summary is not analysis. To understand the reading, you need to look again for key points. (See Chapter 10 on reading and Chapter 12 on understanding themes.) Knowing what you might look for will help you avoid misunderstanding.
Has factual errors.	You misstate or misrepresent some aspect of the text. This does not mean you are misinterpreting—it means you are making faulty references, saying the text says one thing when it doesn't. The only way to fix this is through careful reading. You cannot replace careful reading with skimming. You are not skimming to find an answer to a question—you are reading to gain an in-depth understanding. See Chapter 10.
Makes an unnecessary observation.	You may be giving too much emphasis to a discrete aspect of the text. Instead, base your claims on a broader understanding. In general, do not attribute too much meaning to one word or incident. On the other hand, one word can be critical, especially if it is isolated, or repeated. Learn to see elements of a text in the context of the whole.

Problem *The writer . . .*	Solution/Strategy
Has no real thesis, but instead gives a list of literary terms.	Many times the prompt suggests literary elements to consider in your analysis of the text, but these are means to an end. You must have some reason to mention them. There is no value in pointing out the evocative images in the second stanza if you don't intend to explain why they're important to the poem as a whole.
Fails to address the second poem (or passage).	The AP Lit exam will often provide two texts to consider for a compare/contrast exercise. Most often the texts are poems. If you understand one and not the other, you will earn a low score because you are failing to meet the expectation of the prompt. In any compare/contrast exercise, look for the corresponding ideas, literary elements, and themes. A simple Venn diagram in the margin might help you organize your thoughts.
Presents contradictory claims.	There are two ways to think about this. One is that you lost track of what you were arguing and decided to go a different way, or, more likely, you weren't sure what the passage was about and you're struggling with meaning. I can't stress enough how important it is to do a careful reading, so you know what you want to argue. Then, a mini-outline should help you avoid obvious contradictions in your own thinking.

Test Tip

If you have six claims you can argue in your essay, pick the best three or four. Depth, not breadth, is what is called for.

C: YOU MISREAD THE PROMPT

Problem *The writer . . .*	*Solution/Strategy*
Is completely off topic.	You perhaps charged too quickly out of the starting gate, with your eyes on the finish line instead of on your strategy for winning. You will not earn a high score if you're writing a different essay than the one you're expected to write. The prompt is carefully written to guide you. Use it. Read it several times. Underline the actual task. (See Chapter 14 for more help with this.)
Focuses on the wrong elements.	If the prompt lists specific literary elements to consider, pay attention to that list. The exam writers are telling you that these elements are at work in the text. If you go off on your own, you risk a limited or wrong analysis. On the other hand, they may be testing your ability to choose the most significant literary devices in a text from the list given. If you focus on the wrong choice, you risk a lower score. The key to choosing the right elements is prevalence or dominance. The more the literary element aids the writer in his or her purpose, the more you can write about it.
Has gone off topic and failed to connect with the main intent of the prompt.	According to the College Board, "prompts evolve from passages and are written to stimulate and open up discussion, not provide closure." However, once stimulated, your mind cannot journey somewhere unrelated to the prompt, as that will be seen as a misreading.

In choosing literary elements to consider for your essay, remember that in analyzing poetry, it will be rare that the rhyme scheme has any effect at all. While it is easy to determine a rhyme scheme, what will you say about its effect? It is not enough to identify literary elements. You must also show how they function in a literary work.

D: IMPRECISE USE OF LANGUAGE; IMPRECISE UNDERSTANDING OF LITERARY ELEMENTS

Problem *The writer . . .*	*Solution/Strategy*
Identifies techniques imprecisely.	If you say, for example, "flowy" instead of fluent, you are showing a lack of scholarship. You must have a good knowledge of at least the basic literary terms (see Chapter 6). If you do not have the words to say what you mean, you will struggle and your score will reflect that.
Uses simplistic vocabulary.	One unstated aspect of your writing that AP readers are looking at is your ability to use sophisticated vocabulary. Your essay needs to show and make evident both your understanding of a wide range of words and your ability to use them effectively. One should never stick in "fancy" words for the sake of doing so. Choosing the exact word for the job is part of being a writer. If your own word choice is limited, your ability to express yourself may also be limited. (See Chapter 9 for more on vocabulary.)

GENERATING YOUR ANALYSIS

Step one: Read the prompt carefully.

Understand exactly what you are expected to do. This will give you a purpose for reading. If the prompt asks you, for example, to analyze the effect of an event on a character, then be looking exactly for that as you read. The prompt may or may not provide a short list of possible literary elements or devices that you can consider in analyzing how the writer achieves his or her purpose. When you read the passage or poem (step two), mark those devices and simultaneously be thinking how they help the author convey the effect of experience on the character.

Step two: Read the poem or prose passage carefully.

If you skim, you are not going to have a good understanding of what you've read and will, therefore, have nothing intelligent to say. The essay section counts for 55% of your cumulative score, so it seems logical that you'd want to give the three essays your best effort.

Don't think that skimming the reading will save you time. In the long run, you'll be at a huge disadvantage. Instead, use the tips in Chapter 10 on engaged and active reading to help you read both quickly and deeply. As you read, annotate the text, marking significant aspects of the text as they relate to the task laid out in the prompt.

Step three: Create a **mini outline**.

In the margin of your test page (the one with the prompt on it), draft a quick thesis and outline several main claims in support of your thesis. Use symbols to connect those prompts to corresponding evidence in the text. For example, give claim #1 a star and put stars by everything in the text that relates. You may not use it all in your essay, but identifying it is an important step in creating a well-organized and detailed analysis.

Step four: Write your essay.

Begin writing your essay. Be sure to minimize the effect of biases, be mindful of your word choices, and be sure your points are well argued. (See Chapter 15 for more on essay writing.) Be sure to use the outline you created to keep you focused. However, if you discover something you didn't see before as you write, and you are sure that the new discovery is important, pay attention to it. Do not be too constrained by your initial outline.

CSE: A FORMULA TO REMEMBER

Remember "CSE" and you'll remember the main elements of a good argumentative essay:

C State a **claim**

S **Support** that claim
with evidence from the text

E **Explain** your thinking

See more about CSE in Chapter 15.

As you are writing, if you discover something you didn't see before, and you are sure that the new discovery is important, pay attention to it. Do not be too constrained by your initial outline.

So What? Understanding Literary Themes

OVERVIEW

Each summer, my AP students read Jostein Gaarder's novel of the history of Western philosophy, *Sophie's World*. They read it so we can begin our year of literary study with a better understanding of the key questions that have concerned human beings for all of recorded history—questions like "Who am I?," "Is there life after death?," and my personal favorite, "How ought we to live?" The questions that drive philosophers are almost always the same questions that drive writers. Truly great works of literature are always about something—there is always a point. And the point, the "so what" in a significant work of literature is going to be a theme that is universal and timeless. It will be found to be true for all people of all times and in all places.

WHAT IS "SO WHAT?"

To write a good essay for the AP Lit exam, you must discover the thematic truth in the poem and prose text that you are given. This is the point—the theme that you must look for when you read the passage. Not everyone will see the same thing in a work, but the texts chosen for each exam do have important ideas in them. You will always be asked to "zoom in" on that important idea, the thing I call the "So What." In other words, when I read a poem, I ask "So what?" What is it about this poem that really matters? What is the point that the writer is trying to make?

Once you discover that underlying idea, then you'll analyze **the ways the poet or author reveals that theme** to readers through a variety of literary elements. It will never be enough to simply recognize figurative language or imagery. If that is all you do, the reader of your essay may also ask, "So what?"

Therefore, "So What" can be viewed in two ways:

1. the universal theme of a poem or prose text;

2. your insight into that theme as revealed through your careful analysis of literary elements.

This universal theme or truth must drive your essay. Without it you are writing about nothing. Without it, your reader will ask, "So what?"

SO WHAT? A VISUAL GUIDE*

So What is the Why.

So What?

So What is the true meaning of a story.

...there is always a point.

So What is what makes a piece of literature matter. It is what makes it full, not flat.

The author is saying something that is universally true.

There is universal meaning in the passage, something that relates to real life.

The writer refers to both the writer of the literary passage and the student writer who is struggling to make meaning of the text.

There is no reason for an essay without a So What.

The universal truth the writer (student) will explain.

The So What is the unifying idea that keeps the writer (student) on track. Without it, you can forget why you're writing in the first place.

The So What of an essay is the point the writer is trying to make.

Without it, [a student's essay] will prompt the reader to say, "so what. What is the significance of this essay."

The So What statement is located in the [student's] introduction, but it should also be apparent throughout the essay. It should drive the essay.

It is a universal truth that everyone can learn from or relate to.

It is the profound message that the author is trying to get the reader to understand--often a moral or a life lesson.

*This visual guide was created with help from the author's 2010 AP English Literature class.

COMMON LITERARY THEMES

THEMATIC STATEMENTS:

- All life is connected.
- Each life, no matter how small, matters.
- Life is too brief.
- Youth (innocence) and beauty don't last.
- We don't appreciate what we have until it's gone.
- Pride can blind us to the truth.
- Small acts of kindness and/or generosity can have a tremendous effect.
- Courage can reward those who push themselves.
- Sometimes we learn too late what we need to know.
- Social status, beauty, wealth, etc., do not matter.
- We learn through trial, hardship, or pain those lessons most valuable.
- The individual is sometimes in conflict with society.
- Individuals are often alienated and alone.
- Self-determination is a fierce inner force, but is often thwarted or delayed by outside forces.
- Fantasy is sometimes more real than everyday reality.
- Mortality (death) is inevitable.
- Human beings are sometimes too weak (or too blind) to do what is right.
- We often want what others have or we often want what we cannot have.
- Fear, jealousy, and greed are destructive emotions.

- We sometimes hurt those we love.

- People (of all cultures and of all times) are more alike than they are different.

- Nature does not care about people.

- Each of us is alone (often feeling small or frightened) in the world.

- Evil exists in the hearts of men (women).

THEMATIC QUESTIONS:

- What is truth?

- What is beauty?

- What is real?

- What is justice?

- What is honor?

- What is love?

- What does it mean to live a good life?

- What does it mean to be a hero?

- What does it mean to have courage?

Make a card listing your top ten literary themes and carry it with you. Look at it often. Make these themes serve as the lens through which you view the world. You will start to hear these themes in songs, see them in movies, and even recognize them on TV shows. More importantly, you will be better able to recognize them in the literature you read. The result of "practicing" themes is that when you read those complex passages and poems on the AP Lit exam, you will be able to recognize the "so what" quickly.

Point of View:
From Whose Perspective?

"You never really understand a person until you consider things from his point of view."

—Atticus Finch in Harper Lee's *To Kill a Mockingbird*

OVERVIEW

There are two main ways to consider point of view: the point of view in the passage that you are to identify and your own point of view as you consider the passage and what it means. This chapter will help you to realize the importance of both.

YOUR OWN POINT OF VIEW

An inherent disadvantage to youth is that it comes with a limited world view. Most high school students have limited life experience. We cannot blame them for this, but as experience affects one's ability to conceive of complex literary themes, it is a matter worth addressing here. In addition, each of us, despite our age, can work to broaden our experience so we can have an even fuller world view.

In addition to your age, your point of view is influenced by your

- culture: ethnicity, religion, etc.

- environment: urban, rural, specific region of the country

- family values

- economic status

- actual life experiences: travel, personal interactions with people who are different from you, even having been in love

These influences cause us to have particular biases. Everyone has biases. It is important for us to recognize that fact and understand that our point of view and our biases affect how we read. To be good critical readers, we must control and limit the effect of our biases.

CONSCIOUSLY AND PURPOSEFULLY ADD TO WHAT YOU KNOW ABOUT LIFE

One of the best ways to understand literature and its themes is to read. But sometimes we need to have experiences that help us understand what we read. To do this, consider expanding your knowledge of the world in the following ways:

- Engage in conversations with people from different cultures
- Talk to older adults about their life experiences
- Add variety to your media preferences:
  - read a variety of books (see Chapter 4)
  - listen to different types of music
  - watch foreign films, with subtitles
  - read national and international newspapers
  - watch The History Channel
  - download lectures and philosophy podcasts and listen to them (*iTunes U* is a fantastic resource for free materials at a college level)

BECOME AN EMPATHETIC READER

Empathy is *the ability to put ourselves in someone else's place, to see things as he or she sees them.* As readers, we must be empathetic if we are to truly understand the characters in the books we read. To do this, it means you have to actually put yourself in the place of the speaker, the narrator, or the character.

When you read, visualize yourself in the text. Make a "mind movie" in which you walk through the setting, follow the characters, listen to them speak, and observe their actions. Even more importantly, allow yourself to feel what the character feels. This is empathy.

Many questions on the AP Lit exam ask you to determine the attitude or the reaction of a character or speaker to an event. If you become an empathetic reader, this task will be much easier for you.

The more you practice empathetic reading, the more you will develop a kind of "double vision," in which you'll view the text from both within and without, as a critical reader who sees the parts as they relate to the whole.

In your double vision, you'll learn to appreciate how the writing conveys enduring and universal ideas through the perspective of a character, narrator, or speaker.

THE IMPORTANCE OF IRONY AND TONE

Many AP readers say that students have difficulty recognizing irony in passages on the exam. Questions about irony are prevalent in the multiple-choice section. Recognizing irony is an aspect of seeing clearly. If something is not what it seems, perhaps there is something ironic. But more than that, you will need to determine the effect the ironic passage has in the text as a whole.

Dramatic irony is a powerful tool authors employ to reveal thematic insight. Whenever you know something a character or speaker does not know or is not aware of, you should make note of the discrepancy in the margin of the text. As you follow your character around in your "mind movie," pay attention to moments when you feel smarter or more aware than he is. What does that show you?

A character's speech is not always meant to be taken literally. Watch for **verbal irony** *when what a character says is different from what she really means*. The voice may even be sarcastic. Look for the underlying truth and how that truth functions in the text.

Lastly, watch for evidence of **situational irony**. This can be *a discrepancy in the setting or situation that is not what you expect*. For example, you'd not expect a very wealthy widow to be eating cat food. What might that detail mean?

TONE

Tone is *the writer's attitude toward the writing itself; toward the subject; toward the people, places, time and events in the passage and/or toward the audience.* Tone is an important tool in understanding what the writer is saying. The writer's tone or attitude may be serious, humorous, sarcastic, ironic, pessimistic, critical, objective, or playful. Indeed, the author's feelings may be any of the attitudes and feelings that human beings experience. The author will create a specific tone that reinforces how the narrator, speaker, or character feels about someone or something. The author's style reveals these attitudes to the reader. When you are asked to determine the speaker's reaction to an event, look for the underlying emotions in any passage.

REVIEWING MAIN POINTS OF VIEW

- **First person:** the narrator tells his/her own story using first person pronouns. This point of view is limited by what the narrator can know, see, or understand. First person narrators cannot always be trusted to assess the situation honestly. They may be blind to their own faults, etc.

- **Second person:** the narrator uses second person pronouns to make immediate connections with readers (a very rare point of view in fiction).

- **Third person-limited:** a third person narrator tells the story (generally the main character's story, but sometimes tells the story from a peripheral character's viewpoint) using third person pronouns. A third person limited narrator is similar to a first person narrator in that he can only see and know what his character can see and know.

- **Third person-omniscient:** this third person narrator is god-like, seeing and knowing all without constraints of time or space, seeing even beyond earthly existence. Third person narrators often digress into contemplative or philosophical forays. Third person omniscient narrators will often voice the viewpoint of the author.

- **Objective:** an objective narrator tells a story like a video recorder would, simply revealing the sights and sounds it perceives (though not, of course, as strictly as that). Recognize an objective narrator by that person's lack of emotion or personal interest in the subject.

Test Tip

Remember, you can't always trust a first person narrator. Be a careful and critical reader, and you'll know what she does not know.

SHIFTS IN POINT OF VIEW

A shift in point of view is something to pay close attention to. It is often a critical marker in understanding meaning or theme. Use the following list of questions as your guide:

1. Identify the shift. Where does it occur? From whose point of view to whose?

2. Why does the shift occur? What can the author accomplish with this new narrative point of view?

3. What changes are evident in narrative style, narrative voice, even syntax and diction?

4. What can you see that you did not see before? Something new? Something different? Something opposite?

5. What limitation exists?

6. What does this new "viewer" know that the previous one did not? Or vice versa.

7. What is the overall effect of this shift?

Pull all of your observations together to create a defensible claim for an essay.

POINT OF VIEW IN YOUR ESSAY

Literary present tense

Characters in a novel live in the present time in the novel. To write about them, we use what is called the literary present tense. Atticus *is* a great father to Scout and Jem. Oedipus *plugs* his ears with wax so he won't *hear* the Siren's song. Be cautious when you weave in text citations that are primarily in the past tense. You need to create sentences that are clear and correct. Mixing verb tenses can be very confusing. If you must change the tense in a quoted passage, use [brackets] around the parts you change.

Authoritative third person

A literary analysis essay like the ones you write for the AP Lit exam are best written in third person, which gives you an authoritative voice. You are writing from your own view, so the tendency is to want to qualify your opinions by adding phrases such as "I think," "I feel," and "In my opinion." It is actually better to avoid such qualifiers. Instead write strong, confident claims that sound as if they are fact. It will be your task to support your claims well so that your reader accepts your opinions, but don't intentionally limit them with qualifying phrases. Think of how you respond to the examples below. Which one of each pair seems stronger, more like a fact?

Qualified Claim	Authoritative Claim
In my opinion, Scout learns that being a lady is about honor and integrity, not dresses.	Scout learns that being a lady is about honor and integrity, not dresses.
When Juliet warns Romeo to "swear not by the moon, the inconstant moon/That monthly changes in her circled orb" I think she means that	When Juliet warns Romeo to "swear not by the moon, the inconstant moon/That monthly changes in her circled orb" she means that . . . .

Universal first person

In general we use third person in literary analysis essays. However, there are times when first person seems perfectly correct for the point we want to make. We use universal first person when we include ourselves in all the masses who understand universal truths or themes. We'll use "we" instead of "I" to show our alliance in a common understanding or purpose. It may be appropriate to use the universal first person point of view, especially in your essay's conclusion if you extend your theme as something we all know or should know.

PART IV:
ESSAY INSIGHTS

Free-Response Questions:
A Prompt Analysis

OVERVIEW

The purpose of this chapter is to give you a summary of the types of prompts that have appeared on previous AP Lit exams. Free-response prompts tend to have some consistent qualities. Knowing these qualities can help you to be prepared for your own exam day.

THREE TYPES OF FREE-RESPONSE QUESTIONS

1. A prose passage is provided (generally fiction, but sometimes nonfiction) for you to read and write about.

2. A poem (or two for comparison) is provided for you to read and write about.

3. A general question is provided along with a list of possible works that fit the prompt. It is up to you to choose the work that is the best fit for the question. You <u>must</u> choose a work you know well. It <u>must</u> be a work of literary merit (see Chapter 4).

PROMPTS, IN GENERAL

An essay prompt does several things:

1. Asks you to carefully read a specific text.

2. Gives you a content task to accomplish (see examples later in this chapter).

3. Gives you a hint about the main theme of a passage or poem or openly states a theme for the open-ended question (question #3).

4. May, or may not, give you a brief list of literary elements to consider in your argument.

5. Directly tells you to write a well-organized essay.

For example, let's analyze the prose prompt from the 1994 released exam:

Prompt	Analysis
"Read the following passage carefully. Then write an essay **showing how the author dramatizes the young heroine's adventure**. Consider such literary elements as diction, imagery, narrative pace, and point of view."	**Content task:** "[show] how the author dramatizes the young heroine's adventure.
	Lit elements to consider are given: diction, imagery, narrative pace, and point of view.
	Notes:
	As you read the passage, you need to understand the heroine's adventure. What is it? Why is it an adventure? How is it dramatic, or dramatized?
	The writers of this prompt suggest that you also consider the author's choice of words, imagery, narrative pace, and point of view.
	These are more than suggestions—they are strong hints. Don't ignore them!
	In fact, this text includes an interesting shift in point of view that would be a mistake to ignore. You will need to determine the effect of that shift.
	Also, it's not enough to pick out strong images or great word choices. You must show how these elements help the author dramatize the young heroine's adventure.

Test Tip

It is critically important for you to know exactly what a prompt is asking for and respond appropriately. You will earn a very low score if you fail to do what the prompt asks you to do.

Find more prompts from released exams online at AP Central (*http://apcentral.collegeboard.com/apc/public/exam/exam_questions/index.html*). This is a valuable website to help you study.

ANALYSIS OF PROSE PASSAGE PROMPTS

The information that follows comes from an analysis of approximately 25 prose prompts from released exams.

Content Task	Key Elements
Analyze the style and tone of the passage, explaining how they help to express the author's attitudes.	style/tone author's attitude
Discuss the ways the author differentiates between the writing of (author one) and that of (author two).	compare two texts
Analyze the narrative techniques and other resources of language the author uses to characterize a mother and the mother's attitudes toward her daughter.	characterization characters' attitudes
Define the author's view and analyze how he conveys it.	characterization
Show how the author dramatizes a young heroine's adventure.	characterization
Analyze how the author uses literary techniques to characterize _____	characterization
Analyze how the narrator reveals the character of _____.	characterization
Analyze how changes in perspective and style reflect the narrator's complex attitude toward the past.	narrator's attitude

Content Task	Key Elements
Write an essay in which you characterize the narrator's attitude toward _____ and analyze the literary techniques used to convey this attitude.	narrator's attitude characterization
Show how the author's techniques convey the impact of the experience on the main character.	characterization
Analyze how the language of the passage characterizes the diarist and his society and how the characterization serves _____ satiric purpose.	characterization compare/contrast analysis of satire
Analyze the techniques that the author uses to characterize _____ and _____.	characterization compare/contrast
Analyze how the author produces a comic effect.	narrative effect, comedy
Analyze how the author's use of language generates a vivid impression of _____ as a character.	characterization general use of language
Explain how the author uses narrative voice and characterization to provide a social commentary.	social commentary characterization narrative voice
Analyze the author's depiction of the three characters and the relationships among them.	characterization compare/contrast
Analyze how the author uses elements such as point of view, selection of detail, dialogue, and characterization to make a social commentary.	elements of literature social commentary

Continued →

(Continued from previous page)

Content Task	Key Elements
Show how the author uses literary devices to achieve her purpose.	The task is vague, perhaps on purpose. In this case, you'd be expected to determine the author's purpose first.
Discuss how the characterization in the passage reflects the narrator's attitude toward _____.	characterization narrator's attitude
Analyze how the playwright reveals the values of the characters and the nature of their society.	point of view of characters characterization of society
Discuss how the narrator's style reveals his attitudes toward the people he describes.	narrator's attitude characterization
Analyze how the author uses techniques to characterize the relationship between a young man and his father.	characterization
Analyze how the author uses literary devices to characterize _____ experience.	characterization point of view of character
Analyze how the author establishes _____ relationship to the urban setting.	characterization point of view of character analysis of elements of literature: setting
Analyze the literary techniques the author uses to describe _____ and to characterize the people who live there.	analysis of elements of literature: setting

LITERARY TECHNIQUES/DEVICES

Exam writers sometimes list literary techniques or devices in the passage prompts for you to consider. The most prevalent are listed below. Be aware, though, that frequently no list is given. In those cases, you are expected to discover, on your own, which literary elements are at work in the passage.

Prevalence Rating

★ = 1–2 instances   ★★ = 3–5 instances   ★★★= 6+ instances

Diction ★★	Selection of detail ★★★
Dialogue/speech ★	Structure ★
Figurative language ★★	Style ★
Imagery ★★	Syntax ★★★
Narrative pace ★	Tone ★★★
Point of view ★	The prompt gives no list of literary devices ★★★
Repetition ★	

ANALYSIS OF POETRY PROMPTS

The information that follows come from an analysis of poetry prompts from released exams. About one-third of the free-response prompts for poetry ask you to compare elements in two poems.

Content task	Key Elements
Show how the use of language reveals the speaker's attitude toward _____.	speaker's attitude
Trace the speaker's changing responses to his experience and explain how they are conveyed by the poem's diction, imagery, and tone.	speaker's response/ attitude changes/shifts
Discuss how such elements as language, imagery, structure, and point of view convey meaning.	vague allusion to theme: would need to determine meaning on your own
Considering such elements as speaker, diction, imagery, form, and tone, write a well-organized essay in which you contrast the speakers' views of _____.	compare/contrast speakers' point of view
Analyze how the speaker uses the imagery of the poem to reveal his attitude toward _____.	speaker's attitude
Discuss how the poem's controlling metaphor expresses the complex attitude of the speaker.	speaker's attitude
Explain how formal elements such as structure, syntax, diction, and imagery reveal the speaker's response to _____.	speaker's response (point of view)
Analyze how the poem reveals the speaker's complex conception of _____.	speaker's point of view

Content task	Key Elements
Explain how the poet conveys not just a literal description of _____ but a deeper understanding of the whole experience.	poet's point of view
Compare the portrayals of the _____.	compare/contrast
Analyze how the author uses elements such as allusion, figurative language, and tone to convey the speaker's complex response to his dismissal from court.	speaker's point of view
Analyze how the poet employs literary devices in adapting the Greek myth to a contemporary setting.	compare/contrast
Analyze how the poet uses language to portray the scene and convey mood and meaning.	analysis of setting, mood
Discuss how the poet uses literary techniques to reveal the speaker's attitude toward _____ and _____.	speaker's attitude
Compare and contrast two poems, analyzing the significance of _____ in each of the poems.	compare/contrast analysis of setting
Analyze the techniques the poet uses to develop the relationship between the speaker and the setting.	speaker's point of view analysis of setting

LITERARY TECHNIQUES/DEVICES

Exam writers sometimes list literary techniques or devices in the poetry prompt for you to consider. The most prevalent are listed below. Be aware, though, that frequently, no list is given. In those cases, you are expected to discover, on your own, which literary elements are at work in the passage.

Prevalence Rating

★ = 1–2 instances   ★★ = 3–5 instances   ★★★ = 6+ instances

Allusion ★	Repetition ★
Diction ★★★	Selection of detail ★★★
Figurative language ★★	Sound (rhythm, rhyme) ★
Form ★	Structure ★★
Imagery ★★★	Syntax ★
Language (general) ★	Tone ★★
Narrative pace ★	The prompt gives no list of literary devices ★★★
Point of view ★	

Start reading a lot of poems. For each one, determine what the speaker's attitude is and how you know it. Knowing the speaker's attitude about someone or something is one of the main tasks given in poetry prompts.

ANALYSIS OF OPEN-ENDED PROMPTS

The information that follows comes from an analysis of open-ended prompts from released exams. The themes are paraphrased to give you a summary view.

Nearly all of the prompts warn you to <u>avoid</u> plot summary. They also expect you to choose an appropriate work of literary merit. "Appropriate" means that you can defend your thesis by references to that work.

Main Thematic Focus	Main Literary Focus
Show how a character's alienation reveals the surrounding society's assumptions and moral values.	character's conflict
Show how a character is caught between colliding cultures — national, regional, ethnic, religious, institutional.	character's conflict
Analyze how tension between outward conformity and inward questioning contributes to the meaning of a work.	analysis of elements of literature: theme
Show how a specific death scene helps to illuminate the meaning of a work.	analysis of elements of literature: theme
Choose a character whose private passion conflicts with his or her responsibilities. In your essay show the nature of the conflict, its effects upon the character, and its significance to the work.	character's conflict
Show the author's purpose for including a struggle for dominance.	author's style/technique

Continued ➝

(Continued from previous page)

Main Thematic Focus	Main Literary Focus
Choose an important character who is a villain. Then analyze the nature of the character's villainy and show how it enhances meaning in the work.	analysis of elements of literature character
Explain how a scene or scenes of violence contribute to the meaning of the complete work.	analysis of elements of literature: theme
Analyze the sources of a conflict between a parent and a son or daughter and explain how the conflict contributes to the meaning of the work.	character's conflict
Show how the presentation of a character considered evil or immoral creates more sympathy in us than would normally be expected.	analysis of elements of literature character
Describe how an author gives mental or psychological events, such awakenings or discoveries as sense of excitement, suspense or climax.	author's style/technique
Show how the author's manipulation of distinct elements of time contributes to the effectiveness of the work as a whole.	author's style/technique
Show how a morally ambiguous character plays a pivotal role in a work and how his or her moral ambiguity is significant to the work as a whole.	analysis of elements of literature: character
Select a tragic figure who functions as an instrument of suffering in others and explain how the suffering contributes to the tragic vision of the work as a whole.	analysis of elements of literature: character

Main Thematic Focus	Main Literary Focus
Choose a scene or character that creates thoughtful laughter in the reader and show why this laughter is thoughtful and how it contributes to the meaning of the work.	analysis of elements of literature: setting or character
Show how the opening scene of a play or the first chapter of a novel introduces some of the major themes of the work.	analysis of elements of literature: structure
Show how a wedding, funeral, party, or other social occasion reveals the values of the characters and the society in which they live and discuss the contribution the scene makes to the work.	analysis of elements of literature: setting/scene
Show how a character who appears briefly, or does not appear at all, is a significant presence in a work, explaining how he or she functions in the work.	analysis of elements of literature: character
Many stories are about an individual who opposes the will of the majority. Select a character who is in opposition to his or her society and discuss the moral and ethical implications for both the individual and the society.	character's conflict
Identify and explain an allusion that predominates a work and analyze how it enhances the meaning.	author's style/technique

Continued →

(Continued from previous page)

Main Thematic Focus	Main Literary Focus
Show how the character's relationship to the past contributes to the meaning of the work.	character's conflict
Choose a minor character who serves as a foil to a main character and analyze how the relationship between the foil character and the major character illuminates the meaning of the work.	analysis of elements of literature: character
Analyze how a symbol functions in a work and what it reveals about the characters or themes of the work as a whole.	analysis of elements of literature: symbol

Test Tip

Know the basic elements of character: appearance, speech, thoughts, actions, and what others think of him or her. Of these, speech and action sometimes conflict, just as with real people. It is in these discrepancies that the truth emerges.

Essay Basics

"Persuasion is achieved by the speaker's personal character when the speech is so spoken as to make us think him credible."

—Aristotle in *Rhetoric*

OVERVIEW

You will not be required to write the most brilliant essays you've ever written to do well on the AP Lit exam. But you will need to show that you understand the texts, that you can formulate logical, defensible arguments, and that you can write well-organized and insightful essays. Having said that, your essays for the exam will be considered drafts and AP readers are instructed to award points for what students do well. This chapter aims to acquaint you with what you need to know to write the best essays you can.

ABOUT THE ESSAYS

You will be writing three essays in two hours, which gives you approximately 40 minutes for each essay. In this 40 minutes you must read the text, understand it, formulate your thesis, and write a well-developed and well-organized literary analysis essay.

Chapter 14 contains an analysis of essay prompts from released exams. The list describes the kinds of questions that typically guide the AP Lit essays. There is always an essay on a poem (or a comparison of two poems), a prose passage (fiction or nonfiction essay), and finally an open-ended question for which you must supply the text.

TYPICAL PROBLEMS

If you were to ask an AP reader to list some typical mistakes students make in writing their essays, he or she would most likely mention the following:

- no discernible thesis (therefore, no controlling idea)

- a failure to analyze (the writer summarized or paraphrased instead)

- a failure to move from "what" to "how" and "why"

- a failure to support generalizations or claims with evidence from the text

- only poorly developed ideas, with perhaps one or two ideas repeated over and over

- an inability to integrate and embed quotations from the text in complete sentences

- a wordy introduction that was mostly a restatement of the prompt

- a "boring" conclusion that simply restated the thesis or prompt

- some loosely constructed paragraphs that were not unified

- a reliance on the five-paragraph essay, with no real analysis. (Organization without content is not an essay)

- imprecise use of language. (Never use big words to impress—use the exact right word for the job.)

GENERAL QUALITIES OF A GOOD ESSAY

- A relatively short essay with a defensible thesis and a few insightful claims supported with textual evidence is better than a longer essay that is about nothing. (If you don't understand the prompt or the text, your essay will be about nothing.)

- An essay is not a list of separate ideas clumped together.

- An essay is not a summary of the text—it is an argument that you control. (A generalization without support is not an argument.)

- A thesis needs to respond accurately to the task given in the prompt.

- A good essay is well organized, even if it is a draft. It should have discernible parts: introduction, body, and conclusion.

ELEMENTS OF A GOOD INTRODUCTION

- The task given in the prompt must be acknowledged in your introduction.

- The writer's name and the title of the work must be given. (Correct spelling is essential).

- You cannot take time for windy prose meant to engage the reader. The introduction needs to be precise allowing you to jump into your argument.

- Include a thesis that reveals your insightful understanding of the key ideas in the text.

MORE ON THESIS STATEMENTS

A thesis statement is *the sentence where you state your purpose* or what you intend to prove in your essay. If you don't have something to argue, you don't have a thesis. While reading, you must come to some conclusion about the text, something you believe about the text that you can defend and support. Your thesis comes from that. If you have a good thesis statement, it will serve as your guide.

Test Tip

If you need a formula for constructing a solid thesis sentence, try this one: Thesis = statement acknowledging task + statement showing your insightful recognition of theme (your "so what").

It is possible that you may need two sentences to accomplish your thesis presentation. That is perfectly acceptable. However, watch your words and aim toward fewer rather than more words to say what you need to say.

DEVELOPING THE BODY OF THE ESSAY

The body of your essay is *where you argue your thesis*. You will need to make several points or claims that prove your thesis. A good *formula* for developing the ideas in your argument is the "CSE" formula:

1) State a **claim**. (This may be your topic sentence in a paragraph.)

2) **Support** it with evidence from the text.

3) **Explain** your reasoning, especially showing how or why.

As you write practice essays, use a different highlighter for each "CSE" element to be sure you are indeed writing an analysis and not a summary.

MORE ON EXPLAINING YOUR REASONING

Sometimes, you will think that your ideas are clearly stated, when they're actually only implicit (implied). You need to make your ideas explicit, meaning *you need to show exactly how and/ or why what you say is so*. Make connections. Make your ideas transparent. One of the biggest problems in student essays is the existence of too many implied ideas.

If you (or your reader) are still asking the following questions about your essay, you have not fully explained what you mean:

• Why?

• What is important or significant about this idea?

• What does this have to do with the claim?

You should let your essay develop organically from what you know. There is no set number of paragraphs expected for your AP essays, BUT avoid using the five-paragraph formula. It can be too constrictive, and it may have you thinking more about the formula than your ideas. You may have three body paragraphs, but you may have four, five, or even six. Your paragraphs do not have to be the same length either. If you make your point in three sentences and need to move on to the next paragraph, then do so. The next point you make may need seven sentences. Let your argument determine how you write.

WRITING A CONCLUSION THAT INSPIRES: QUALITIES OF A GOOD CONCLUSION

Avoid generic summary conclusions that simply restate the thesis. They're boring, and they rob you of the opportunity to go beyond your analysis of a text to relate your personal insight. While your conclusion should not be personal, your particular insight does come from you and sometimes the conclusion is where your voice is most strong. Still, remember to stay focused on the text.

SOME CONCLUSION TIPS:

- Never introduce a new idea (a new claim) in the conclusion.
- Generally, do not cite the text in the conclusion.
- Remind the readers of the most important concepts of your essay.
- A good conclusion makes the essay feel finished.
- Avoid cliché phrases like "in conclusion," "to sum up," or the like. However, you still need to make a smooth transition to the end of the essay.

"BUT, WHAT IF I RUN OUT OF TIME?"

It is possible that you will not have time to write a conclusion. Of course it is best if you can end with something, even a sentence or two, but in the event that the proctor is standing over you with his hand out, your essay will have to stand without its ending. Do not fret. The introduction and the body are the most crucial parts and should show your insightful analysis. It is possible to score well without a true conclusion.

Test Tip *The best preparation for writing a complete AP Lit essay in 40 minutes is to practice, practice, practice! It takes a lot of effort, but your diligence will be rewarded.*

QUOTING THE TEXT: TIPS AND STRATEGIES

- Use partial quotations. It will be rare that you will need to quote an entire sentence from a text. Use only the part that helps you to prove your point.

- If your essay is mostly quotations from the text, it is not your essay. So, don't over-quote! Your job is not to string together phrases from the text. You are to use phrases from the text to prove your claims.

- Think about why you want to use the quoted phrase or passage in the first place. How does it support your claim? If you don't know, why are you quoting it?

- When quoting the text, set it up. You must give context first. If you find yourself "plopping" in a quotation and then explaining it, you have not provided the context. (See the section below for more help with this).

INTEGRATING OR EMBEDDING (SUPPORT) TEXTUAL EVIDENCE

Weaving textual evidence into an essay is a skill that you can practice and learn to do well. You should study good models. Reading a newspaper can help you. Journalists are experts at integrating quotations into their text. They must attribute quotations to their sources as well. Even though they're not quoting literary texts, they do follow similar guidelines for embedding their quotations.

Learn these rules for integrating your textual support:

- You need to supply context for the full or partial quotation. This means to set it up somehow, or transition into the quotation with your claim.

- As a general rule, don't start the sentence with the quotation.

- Use quotation marks around anything you take from the text, even isolated words.

- When you weave in the cited text, you must end up with a grammatically correct sentence. If you have to change tense or wording, use [brackets] around the parts you change.

- If the quotation or cited text is not self-evident and you must still explain it, why did you include the quotation? What does it show or prove?

- Use slashes (/) to separate lines of poetry from one another.

Some model phrases to consider:

- The writer (poet) or speaker argues, claims that, suggests, etc._____. His description of "_____."

- "_____" reads quickly, even frantically. This narrative pace suggests that _____.

- When _____(author) writes that _____, she shows how "_____."

- The imagery in stanza four contrasts with stanza one. "_____" suggests something, while "_____" is clearly meant to _____.

- _____(Character's name) feels trapped by her situation. She "_____."

- "_____," "_____," and "_____" are words commonly heard in church, which gives the passage _____ .

When you read student essay samples from the AP Central website, look specifically at how the writers of top score essays incorporate evidence from the text to prove their point.

USING PRECISE LANGUAGE: CONFIDENTLY SAYING WHAT YOU MEAN

- Use higher-level vocabulary

  I have suggested that you not toss in "big" words in your essays that you don't know. However, you still need to show that you have a sophisticated vocabulary. Begin to use the words you are learning from your word list in Chapter 9. If you never use a "big" word, your prose may sound simplistic.

- Use strong verbs

  Avoid using "being verbs" or linking verbs, as they do not express action. Instead choose strong, vivid action verbs. Your writing will be more powerful and more visual. When we write with linking and being verbs, we rely too much on adjectives. Adjectives can be vague or ambiguous. See the samples below.

Being/Linking Verbs			
is	are	have been	should have been
am	be	had been	would have been
was	been	shall be	feels
were	being	will be	seems

How do you know if it's an action verb? If you can act it out, it is an action verb. I can act out "dance," but I cannot act out "was."

Check your own writing for strong verb use. Choose any essay and highlight all the linking/being verbs you have used. Then, revise the essay and replace those highlighted verbs with action verbs. Notice the difference in the quality of your essay.

Below are some sample sentences that show the difference between using linking verbs and action verbs. Notice how much more vivid and descriptive the action verbs make the sentences.

Linking Verbs	Action Verbs
Sylvia was clumsy.	Sylvia tripped over the smallest pebble.
The images are interesting.	The images in the first paragraph evoke pity for the narrator.
The simile is effective.	The simile conjures images of wickedness.

WORDS AND PHRASES TO AVOID

Some words are inherently ambiguous. Others are simply meaningless. Others are cliché or overused expressions that are out of place in a scholarly essay. It is best to always avoid words and phrases that promote imprecision.

Avoid using:

- "Very," "really," "completely," etc. Superlatives added to adjectives are generally not needed.

- "Interesting." We all know that saying "that's interesting" can mean so many different things that it can actually mean nothing.

- "This," "that" and "it" can be ambiguity traps. It's best to not use them. For example: "That is why he never told even his closest friends about it." What is "that?" Furthermore, what is "it?"

- "Like," as in "the character was so like suffocated by his mother's dreams for him." Watch out for speech dysfluencies in writing. You are writing, not speaking.

- "Talks about" as in "This passage talks about." Passages do not talk. Instead say, the author writes, shows, reveals, etc.

- "Wonderful," "skillfully," "fantastic," when meant to compliment the writer. Do not "suck up" to the writer. This gains you no points. Praising the prose is not analyzing the prose.

NEVER, NEVER …

- Begin a sentence with a pronoun.

- Begin a paragraph with a pronoun.

- Use ambiguous pronouns: this, that, those, it, etc.

- Write like you speak. That is, do not use a conversational style that screams out: "I am not serious."

- Use words you do not understand. If you misuse a word, you will lose credibility.

- Use more words than you need to use to make your point.

AVOID CLICHÉS, TRITE EXPRESSIONS, AND REDUNDANT PHRASES

If you've heard it before, it may be a cliché. Clichés are empty expressions that may have been clever at one time, but now simply distract from your writing. If you rely on clichés, you are avoiding your job as a writer, which is to use precise language to say what you mean.

A few common clichés:

- A close call
- A fish out of water
- At wit's end
- Bird's eye view
- Coming down the pike
- Fall on deaf ears
- Never a dull moment
- Nerve wracking
- Nipped in the bud
- Out of the box
- What goes around comes around
- At the end of the day

Redundant phrases:

- "At this point in time": just say *at this point* or *at this time*
- "Cancel out": just say *cancel*
- "Complete opposite": just say *opposite*
- "Each and every": just say *every*

- "Evolve over time": just say *evolve*
- "Join together": just say *join*
- "Look back in retrospect": just say *in retrospect*
- "Nostalgia for the past": just say *nostalgia*
- "Overexaggerate": just say *exaggerate*
- "Past experience": just say *experience*
- "Past history": just say *history*
- "Plan ahead": just say *plan*
- "The reason why": just say *the reason*
- "This day and age": just say *in our time* or *presently*
- "Ultimate goal": just say *goal*

YOUR OWN SYNTAX

You must be able to write effective and fluent sentences for effective prose. Just as the writers whose work is featured on the exam use syntactical patterns, so can you. Study the patterns (see Chapter 5) and learn the value of each. Practice writing various types of patterns. For example, one week, write just simple sentences, the next week compound, etc. This will result in your being able to use anaphora or polysyndeton without even thinking of how to do it, just knowing why you want to do it.

The best way to get better at sentence crafting is to recognize it in the texts you read and then emulate the patterns and effects you see.

Here is an activity to help you to practice writing better
sentences.

Copy-change activity:
*Make a copy of a highly effectively paragraph from a book
and study it. Learn the sentence patterns. Label the sentence
types you see. Then, rewrite the paragraph with a new topic.
Change the nouns and verbs to fit the new topic, but not
their placement. Replicate phrases, clauses, and punctuation
exactly. Learn by imitating.*

YOUR OWN RHETORICAL STRATEGIES

Develop your paragraphs using a variety of rhetorical strategies.
Use what seems appropriate for the text. In other words, you can't
force something that doesn't work. Here are a few basic ways that
you can argue your point.

Exemplification—Use examples from the text to prove
your point. Of course, you will want to choose the best
examples for your purpose.

Process analysis—If you recognize a process (how something
works or operates) in a text, you can identify it and analyze
its elements.

Comparison and contrast—Often, you will be asked to
do this as your main task (such as compare two poems),
but even if you aren't, you may have a reason to show
similarities and differences in another type of question.

Cause and effect analysis—Show why something happens,
the series of events leading to or causing a concluding
event.

TWO TEXTS: A COMPARE/CONTRAST GUIDE

There is a good chance that you will be asked to write an essay comparing the elements of two texts. The following guide is meant to help you to understand the basics of compare/contrast essays.

The texts you will be presented with have some obvious similarities; otherwise, they would not be paired. You may have two poems about a Greek goddess or two descriptive paragraphs about shopping. The subjects will be the same. What will differ will be how the two authors treat the subjects. For example, the attitude of each author toward the subject may be completely different. It will be important for you to understand both overt and subtle similarities and differences. As you read, annotate the text and take marginal notes listing what you find.

Compare means to show similarities.

Contrast means to show differences.

COMPARE/CONTRAST: TRANSITIONAL WORDS AND PHRASES:

To compare

In the same way	Similarly	Like
Likewise	Also	

To contrast

Conversely	Rather	On the other hand
However	On the contrary	

THE INTRODUCTION

Mention both texts and be sure that your thesis suggests the main ways the two texts are similar. Do not say "Jones' poem is similar to Smith's in some ways, but there are also some main differences." Instead say "Even though both poets characterize Venus as powerful, even fierce, Jones gives a sympathetic view of Venus, while Smith warns that her victims will be trapped by love."

THE BODY

Here are three popular methods you can use to organize the body of the essay:

1. With the "Whole to Whole" method you discuss the important aspects of one text, then the other.

   ▸ *You may lose track of your main points if you're not careful.*

2. Another method is to show all similarities, then all of the differences.

   ▸ *This can seem less integrated, less fluent.*

3. You might instead go subject by subject (point by point).

   ▸ *For example you might compare the tone in each poem, then the imagery in each poem, etc.*

ETHOS AND LOGOS: TWO IMPORTANT ARGUMENT "TOOLS"

Aristotle defined qualities of argument centuries ago. Two terms of consequence for you are *ethos* and *logos*.

Ethos: The trustworthiness of the writer. You have to write what you know, what you believe, and support it well. Your essay will be voiceless and powerless if you don't believe in what you are saying.

Logos: Using reason and logic to persuade. You must have a point to argue and know how to do it. You can use the rhetorical strategies listed above.

SAMPLE ESSAY

The following prompt was on the 1994 AP Lit exam.

> *Read the following passage, from "A White Heron" by Sarah Orne Jewett, carefully. Then write an essay showing how the author dramatizes the young heroine's adventure. Consider such literary elements as diction, imagery, narrative pace, and point of view.*

Key words in the prompt are "adventure" and "heroine." The prompt urges you to think of Sylvia's excursion in the old pine tree as a hero's journey. A list of literary elements is given. Diction and imagery are elements of any piece of literature, so those are not unexpected in the list. And while narrative pace and point of view are not uncommon, mentioning them specifically is a hint that they function specifically in this passage.

Find the passage at <http://www.public.coe.edu/~theller/soj/tne/heron.htm> . Look for the first seven paragraphs in part II. The passage begins, "Half a mile from home, at the farther edge of the woods, where the land was highest, a great pine-tree stood, the last of its generation." The passage on the AP Lit exam was abridged from what you find here, but you will have a good sense of what students had as their text for this prompt.

[*Note:* This essay was not scored by AP readers, but is here as a model of an above-average essay.]

In this excerpt from <u>A White Heron</u> by Sarah Orne Jewett[1], the author takes us[2] on an adventurous journey with Sylvia, a small, but far from timid heroine, who shows that courage and tenacity can yield amazing results.[3] Jewett's imagery, diction and shift in point of view create an epic tale of a strong-willed little girl who climbs into a world she has previously only imagined to glimpse the wide world beyond her own[4].

Jewett characterizes Sylvia as a "wistful" child who has long wondered about the old, lone pine tree "the last of its generation[5]," believing that anyone who climbed it could see the ocean. Sylvia is a young heroine with an adventurous spirit who is filled with "wild ambition," a brave girl with "tingling, eager blood coursing the channels of her whole frame." While Sylvia is no stranger to climbing trees, the biggest tree she has previously explored is[6] the white oak whose "upper branches chafed against the pine trunk." She now knows she must go beyond the world she is familiar with and make "the dangerous pass from one tree to the other, so the great enterprise [can] really begin."

While the initial observations of Sylvia's character come through third person omniscient point of view, an interesting shift[7] occurs in the third

---

[1] Always mention title and author in the introduction.

[2] Example of universal first person.

[3] Alludes to the "so what," the universal and enduring theme prevalent in the passage.

[4] Thesis sentence

[5] Integrate only the parts of the text that support your claims. Weave them in so that your sentence is grammatically correct.

[6] Example of literary present tense.

[7] This claim recognizes a shift in point of view: something the prompt hinted would exist.

Overall, notice how the writer makes claims, gives textual evidence to support the claims, and explains what she means.

Evidence from the text can come from anywhere in the text. Quoted passages need not be in the order they were presented in the original text. Writers should use what they need to prove their points.

paragraph when the venerable tree becomes aware of his new tenant. Through the tree's perception of her, we further understand that Sylvia is "determined," "brave," "solitary," and of course "triumphant": all qualities of a hero on a journey.

The pine tree becomes an important character in Sylvia's adventure. He is like a "great main-mast to the voyaging earth," giving the impression that little Sylvia is on the greatest ship of all, sailing into her imagined world. The tree is first wary of his "visitor," who he sees as a "determined spark of human spirit creeping and climbing." But then he comes to appreciate her. While she is in his lower branches, he fights her, but as she continues in her journey, he comes to love his new dependent and even helps her along her way just as a mythical god might have helped humans he cared about; the tree reinforces his "least twigs," making them strong enough to hold her and holds "away the winds" so her last vantage point is steady.

Sylvia's adventure is in some ways comparable to epics of the past, and the lone pine tree provides the setting: it is a foreign land to be explored, full of obstacles, much like the lands beyond Ithaca in which Odysseus found his travails. Jewett's imagery and diction reinforces this idea. Sylvia begins her journey early in the morning "in the paling moonlight," a time when most people are still sleeping. The red squirrel "scolds" her as an unwelcomed stranger in his world. Jewett describes the treacherous climb up a tree that is like a "monstrous ladder," making it seem both tall and menacing. In addition, "sharp, dry twigs caught her and held her and scratched her like angry talons."[8] The trees twigs seem to be attacking Sylvia, like a bird of prey, creating a situation that requires her bravery and perseverance. Weaker spirits may have given up. Further advancing

---

[8] Notice how the writer copes with a shift in verb tense. The text is in past, while this essay is in present tense. Learn to manage this difficulty so your prose is fluent.

The conclusion makes the essay feel complete, but it also reconnects with the "so what."

the idea that Sylvia is in a foreign land, Jewett writes in the third para-graph of the tree's usual inhabitants: "hawks, bats, moths, and sweet-voiced thrushes," creatures that Sylvia would not generally associate with, but now she is in their territory and she can observe them closely.

Then Sylvia reaches the top of the pine tree, nestled in his loving branches. She is at the end of her journey. To see her now from below, she seems like a "pale star," almost as if she's part of heaven instead of earth. Jewett exalts her tiny heroine at last. What Sylvia sees now is tru-ly majestic and a reward for her courage and determination. The golden sun shines on the sea. The hawks are so close that she recognizes how slowly their wings move, and she sees their feathers as gray and "soft as moths," details she never could have detected while on the ordinary earth.

Sylvia's reward is a new view of her own world that may make her feel both small and daring. Like all of us who venture beyond what is familiar and comfortable,[9] she realizes that the world is larger and more vast than she realized. But she must also know that she is ready for any journey her future brings. Unlike more timid spirits, Sylvia's courage and tenacity will reward her with the joys of new discoveries.

---

[9] Sylvia's journey is a metaphor for all of us: push beyond what is familiar and be rewarded for our courage.

Avoid clichés: "comfort zone," "outside the box," etc.

An Analytical Approach to Essay Improvement

"What we have to learn to do, we learn by doing."

—Aristotle

OVERVIEW

In the same way that we learned to ride a bike, or play a piano, or shoot a basket—by repeating the process, by doing it again and again until we understood it—we learned to write by writing. Writing AP essays is a skill you can learn to do well. However, you have to devote time to practice. You cannot learn to write good essays simply by reading this book. This book gives you the guidelines and the tools to use. You must actually <u>practice</u> writing.

STUDYING SAMPLE STUDENT ESSAYS

Every year, the College Board publishes sample student essays for each free-response question. The questions are scored at three levels: high, medium, and low. By recognizing why each essay was scored as it was, you can learn both what to do and what not to do.

The following table is a copy of what you will see when you go to the AP Central website. (Link is given below.) Each item in the cells below will be found at that site. I have numbered each item and explained below what you will find when you click on the link. The information given will vary from year to year. The most important elements are 1, 2, and 5.

2008: FREE-RESPONSE QUESTIONS

Questions	1. All Questions
Scoring	2. Scoring Guidelines
	3. Student Performance Q&A
	4. Scoring Statistics
Samples and Commentary	5. Sample Responses Q1
	Sample Responses Q2
	Sample Responses Q3
Grade Distributions	6. Grade Distributions

1. "All Questions" will take you to the actual questions for that specific year and the texts on which they were based. Often there are two different tests for a given year, which means you have twice as many samples from which to learn. The second test will be labeled *Form B*.

2. "Scoring Guidelines" is a document that the AP readers were given prior to scoring each essay. It is their rubric.

3. "Student Performance Q&A" is a document geared toward AP teachers, but you will find it illuminating as well. The document is a summary of what the intent of each question was, what they were hoping students would do with each question, the average scores, the main problems they witnessed in student essays, and tips for teachers to help students to do better in the future.

4. "Scoring Statistics" shows how most students scored on the essays; it gives you the mean score. Most students typically score in the middle range on their essays.

5. For each question (Q1, 2, and 3) you will get three student essays. There is always a top-rated essay, a middle one, and a lower-rated essay. Look for what makes the top essay different from the middle or lower essay. You will also find a summary of readers' commentaries here. This information can be enlightening, as what they have to say often reinforces what you are learning about writing good essays. Do read and take to heart what they say in the commentary.

6. Sometimes the College Board will publish "Grade Distributions," but not always. This report shows you how many students scored 5's, 4's, and so on. It does not tell you specifically about how students scored on any particular essay, but only for the exam in general. This is the least meaningful bit of information here, and regarding your goal to improve your essays, is not all that helpful.

In your analysis, you will want to specifically look for the following:

1) What did the prompt ask students to do?

2) How effective was the particular student's introduction?

3) How did the writer follow the method of stating a claim, supporting it with evidence from the text, and explaining what he or she meant (CSE)?

4) In high-scoring essays, look for the way the writer introduced quotations and passages from the text.

5) Look for his or her use of transitions from one point to the next, or from the claim to the support.

METHOD FOR ANALYZING SAMPLE STUDENT ESSAYS

The following worksheet was designed to help you to analyze sample student essays for their strengths and weaknesses. By using the worksheet you can see where you need to go with your own writing.

Test Tip

It would be worth your time to repeat this analysis process several times until you clearly see the qualities of top essays versus their less effective counterparts.

The steps of the process are as follows:

Part 1:

1. Read and analyze the prompt for one question. (Don't use question 3 because no text is given for you to read.)

2. Paraphrase the task.

3. Read and annotate the passage.

4. Suggest literary devices, if needed.

5. Write your own introduction, for practice.

6. Write a mini-outline for the essay that you would write —if you were asked to write it.

Part 2:

1. Read and score each of the three essays.

2. Justify your score.

Part 3:

1. Compare your score with the actual score that was given.

2. Read the commentary for each essay.

3. Draw your own conclusions.

You will find everything you need for this exercise at the AP Central site: <http://apcentral.collegeboard.com/apc/members/exam/exam_questions/2002.html>

You may choose any year, but it might be best to start with a recent year to get a prompt that indicates current College Board thinking.

PDF documents you will need to print:

- Click on the "All Questions" link and print (all of the texts and prompts are here).

- Choose one question (not question 3) and print the "Sample Responses" for that question. Do not read this document until told to do so.

- Print "Scoring Guidelines."

[*Note*: You have permission from REA to make copies of the following chart for your personal use.]

PART ONE: UNDERSTANDING THE PROMPT AND YOUR TASK

1. Begin by reading the prompt for any essay question. (Do not use the prompt for question three.) Underline the verbs that direct your task. Circle the thematic focus (the "so-what").

2. Paraphrase the task:

3. Read the passage, annotating it for anything that seems significant, especially in light of the prompt.

4. If your prompt does not suggest literary devices, make a list of what you think are the most important devices here:

5. Practice: Write an introduction as if you were going to write this essay.

6. Create a mini-outline of your main points.

PART TWO: ANALYZING STUDENT SAMPLES

For this part, you will need the "Scoring Guidelines."

Read each of the essays, score each separately, and justify your score (say why you gave each the score you did).

Important!!! Promise not to read the scores or commentaries for each essay until part 3.

Essay # _____

Score: _____

Justification:

Essay # _____

Score: _____

Justification:

Essay # _____

Score: _____

Justification:

PART THREE: COMPARING SCORES

For this part, you will need the commentaries (at the end of the essay document).

Essay #	My Score/ I gave	The Score/ AP readers gave	Observations

PART FOUR: CONCLUSIONS

What did you learn from this analysis?

Summary of Essay Tips

"Mature writing recognizes and explores the ambiguities and ironies that plague human existence."

— Note in the 2007 Student Performance Q&A,
AP Central website

In This Chapter

Overview

Essays in General

Questions 1 and 2

Question 3

OVERVIEW

The purpose of this chapter is to summarize the information found in other chapters of this book and to very specifically reiterate things you must remember. You can be sure that these are important enough to study again and again. The more you remember these tips and strategies and the more you integrate them into how you think about your own writing and thinking processes, the fewer problems you will encounter when writing your essays for the AP Lit exam.

ESSAYS IN GENERAL

- Read the prompt carefully and answer it, attending to all elements of the prompt. Be sure you understand what you are being asked to do.

- It is not necessary (or desirable) to rewrite the prompt on your paper. This wastes your time. Your introduction and thesis will acknowledge that you understand all elements of the prompt.

- Saying the same thing again and again does not strengthen your point.

- An essay can be a draft but it still must be a coherent whole— not a string of disconnected ideas.

- Move from "what" to "why" and "how." Show how literary devices contribute to the meaning of the text.

- Explain fully and support your claims. Do not write in "sound bites."

- Use the literary present tense. Characters in literature are always alive. They live in the present time of the text.

- Avoid second person (you); write primarily in third person, using first as needed (if needed). Third person is a more authoritative voice.

- Never use qualifying phrases like "I think," "I feel," or "In my opinion." The claims you make in your essay belong to no one else but you. Such phrases make you sound less confident.

- Do not present new analysis in the conclusion. The conclusion is meant to provide a finish or end to your essay, not to bring up another point.

- Do not define a literary element. Your readers are fully aware of the meanings of all literary elements.

- Under no circumstances provide a summary of the plot or the action of the work.

QUESTIONS 1 AND 2 (POETRY AND PROSE PROMPTS)

- Some prompts may give you a list of literary elements or techniques to consider for your argument, but some may not. If there is no list, then you are expected to know what literary techniques are significant.

- Do not be a tour guide. Even though the prompt may give you a list of literary elements to explore, it's not your job to take your reader on a tour of the text, pointing out this example of imagery or that metaphor. Instead, focus on one or two elements that are most effective and show how they are effective. This is your analysis.

- Do not write about a literary element if it's not working toward the purpose or effect in the text. For example, rhyme is rarely a significant element in a poem. If you say it is, then it is your job to show how or why.

- Poems are short and therefore students may think simple. However, poems are laden with figurative language. Do not mistake the figurative for the literal. Read poems at least twice to be able to write intelligently.

QUESTION 3 (OPEN-ENDED QUESTION FOR WHICH YOU WILL CHOOSE A NOVEL OR PLAY)

- You must choose a work that fits the question. Choose carefully. Your best choice will probably come from the list of works provided. They are there for a reason—they are all examples of a book or play that fits the question.

- The list of works given for question three is not meant to constrain you and you may choose any other work of equal literary merit. Be very careful in your choice. You will seriously jeopardize your chance of earning a high score if AP readers think the book is not quality literature.

- Do not think that AP readers are unfamiliar with a text you choose. There are hundreds of readers and even if you choose something you think is obscure, someone will be familiar with it.

- Do not use the movie version of a text. You have to read the book (play). If it is clear that you're referring to the movie version, you'll lose points.

- You need to be familiar with details of plot and character. You need to know who's who and their relationships to one another.

- You will be expected to provide specific details from the text. While it is not fair to expect direct quotations, it is fair to expect specific references. Use the graphic organizer in Chapter 4 to record details of plot, character, theme and more for five to seven texts that you know very well. While you won't be able to use these self-made guides on the exam, the act of creating them will help you store what you need to know in your long-term memory.

- A plot summary is not an argument—if you write a summary, you're going to get a very low score.

PART V:

MASTERING THE MULTIPLE-CHOICE SECTION

Chapter

Strategies for Success
on the Multiple-Choice Section

18

"The beginning of knowledge is the discovery of something we do not understand."

—Frank Herbert

In This Chapter

Overview

Strategic Reading

Use the Questions to Take the Test

Tips on Answering Questions

Practice for Real

OVERVIEW

You've been taking standardized tests since you were in elementary school, and no one knows more about test taking than a high school student. However, the stakes for this exam are higher than others you've taken, so it seems appropriate to review the skills and strategies needed to answer multiple-choice questions. Some of what you find in this chapter will seem familiar, as if you've read it in other chapters. But these tips bear repeating.

You will want to have these strategies ingrained in your brain. Just the very nature of the test day can bring stress. You should not have to worry about a "guessing" strategy. Use this chapter in combination with Chapter 19, Types of Multiple-Choice Questions, to ensure your best possible score for the multiple-choice section of the exam.

STRATEGIC READING

Before you answer the first question on the test, you must carefully read passages taken from novels or expository prose or poems. The smart way to read is to <u>read actively</u>. Active reading means that you read with a pen in hand, underlining key ideas, writing notes in the margin, connecting related thoughts and so on. Using your pen actively as you read will help you to be fully focused on what you are reading. It will help you to avoid the distraction that can cause your mind to wander. If you practice active reading, you should only need to read an entire prose text once. However, it is advisable to read poems at least twice. Poetry presents difficulties due to figurative language and indirect expression.

Whether you read a text once or twice, remember to read actively. Use whatever annotation techniques you are comfortable with, but <u>do mark</u> the text as you read. This process of close and active reading will help you remember what you've read and will help you identify key aspects of a particular text.

What to note/mark:

- Circle and link related words. For example, five words with a sarcastic tone in a passage are worth noting.

- Underline key statements (anything that seems to be significant).

- Any shift in speaker, point of view, tone, or purpose is important to note in the margin. Also jot down what you think is happening because of this shift.

- Write your own questions in the margin, even questions as simple as "why?" or "what does this mean?" Your questions help you to think and may be answered as you read further, which will provide a logical link for you.

USE THE QUESTIONS TO TAKE THE TEST

- Test questions may provide insight into the poem/passage and improve your reading comprehension.

- Skimming the test questions before you read can give you a stronger purpose for reading and will help you annotate the text as you read. But do skim quickly. You do not have time to carefully read all the questions first.

TIPS ON ANSWERING QUESTIONS

- While it sounds like common sense, read questions carefully. Be sure you know what a question is asking for. Cursory reading creates careless errors. See chapter 16 for an analysis of question types.

- As a matter of procedure, cross out answers that you know are wrong.

- Many of the really tough questions provide two similar answers that you think are correct. In this case, you must choose the most correct answer. "Most correct" means *the answer is more precise or more detailed.* If another answer is only "sort of" right, then that is most likely not the one to choose.

- Don't overthink a question. Some questions are really, really easy. Many students think such an easy question couldn't possibly be on the exam, so they overthink it and get it wrong.

- If you really don't know the answer, but can eliminate two or more answers, taking a guess might be better than skipping the question. You've already eliminated two answers so you have a 50% chance of guessing right!

- If the question asks you to identify ironic elements, the statement in the answer will reveal the irony. In other words, the answer itself will sound ironic.

- For EXCEPT questions, look for the one thing that doesn't match the others.

- Many questions are going to require a rereading of lines or paragraphs from the text. Do not avoid this step. Your notes and markings of the text should help you navigate the text more efficiently as you reread.

PRACTICE FOR REAL

After reading and studying this book, you might want to get some AP test experience by taking a free AP English Literature and Composition practice test offered by REA, publisher of this book. Go to www.rea.com/crashcourse to access the bonus online test.

After taking the practice exam, analyze your results. When you look back at your answers, ask yourself two questions:

1. Why did I get it right?

2. Why did I get it wrong?

It is just as important for you to understand what you got right as well as what you got wrong. If any topics seem particularly difficult for you, review them now. Study this Crash Course along with your textbook and you'll be all set when test day rolls around.

Test Tip

Look through the practice exam for literary terms you were not familiar with or words you did not understand. Add them to your "to do" list and learn them.

Types of Questions in the Multiple-Choice Section

OVERVIEW

The following information comes from an analysis of four re-leased AP Lit exams. Questions are organized according to pur-pose. The prevalence rating should help you focus your study. The more prevalent the type of question, the more likely you are to see questions like it on your exam.

PREVALENCE RATING

★ = 1–5 instances

★★ = 6–10 instances

★★★= 11+ instances

BASIC QUESTION TYPES

1. All of the following EXCEPT _____ .(★★)

   Be sure to recognize this type of question and carefully consider which answer is not like the others.

2. I only

   I and II

   I, II, and III, etc. (★)

   These can be tricky and time consuming. They were more prevalent on older tests. You are expected to reread and make an informed decision.

3. Double Answers (★★★)

   Answer choices are given in pairs, such as "reverent and aware," "morbid and fascinating." Often the pairs contain one element that cannot be correct.

If one part of a double answer is wrong, the entire thing is wrong.

TYPES OF QUESTIONS BY PURPOSE

GENERAL ANALYSIS QUESTIONS:

1. Determine the purpose or function or rhetorical purpose — of a sentence or phrase or clause or word. (★★★)

2. Draw a general conclusion or make an inference or logical deduction — from a line or group of lines or word(s). (★★★)

3. Determine the effect of the speaker or character's attitude. The variations of this question include analysis of speaker's beliefs, assumptions, and perceptions. (★★★)

4. Determine an element of characterization: how a person, thing, idea, etc., is characterized. (★★★)

5. Give a general interpretation or conclusion. These questions test your general reading comprehension. (★★)

6. Which lines are closest in meaning to or are the best restatement of a phrase or group of lines? (★★)

7. Determine the primary effect or purpose or rhetorical function of a passage or section. (★)

8. Identify the central rhetorical strategy used in the passage. (★)

9. Determine the effect of a rhetorical shift. (★)

ORGANIZATION AND STRUCTURE QUESTIONS:

1. Identify compared/contrasted elements. The question is often worded, "Which best contrasts with _____." The question may also ask you to determine the effect of the contrast or comparison. These compare/contrast questions are often layered with other question types. (★★★)

2. Identify a method of organization in a passage or paragraph. (★)

3. Identify a critical transition point and its effect. (★)

4. Identify a cause/effect relationship in the passage or paragraph. (★)

5. Give an analysis of the relationship between structural elements, such as paragraphs, lines, or sections. (★)

SENTENCE AND SYNTAX QUESTIONS:

1. Give an analysis of syntactic patterns or sentence effects. (★)

2. Give an analysis of repetition elements. (★)

GRAMMATICAL CONSTRUCTION QUESTIONS:

1. Make a grammatical connection, such as "the word or phrase refers to _____." On occasion you are asked to find a word's antecedent. (★★★)

2. Identify what it is that a phrase or clause modifies. (★)

DENOTATION AND CONNOTATION QUESTIONS:

1. Determine, in context, the meaning of a word or phrase. The question is often worded this way: "In context, the word is best interpreted to mean _____." (★★★)

2. Which is the best interpretation of a phrase? (★)

3. Determine the effect of the diction. (★)

LITERARY ANALYSIS QUESTIONS:
(See Chapter 5 for lists of key literary terms)

1. Directly identify a literary element or determine the effect of a particular literary element. (★★)

2. Determine the effect of imagery or a description. (★★)

3. Analyze an element of figurative language. (★★)

4. Determine the effect of an allusion. (★)

5. Determine the mood or tone of a passage or phrase. (★)

6. Identify the literary period. (★)

7. Identify the poetic form. (★)

8. Determine the ironic elements. (★)

9. Identify the style of a paragraph. (★)